AMERICA: THE VIEW FROM EUROPE

Vtopiae Insvlae Figvra by Ambrosius Holbein. (Illustration of the island of Utopia in the original edition of Sir Thomas More's *Utopia*.)

America: The View From Europe

J. MARTIN EVANS

The Portable Stanford Series

SAN FRANCISCO BOOK COMPANY, INC.
San Francisco 1976

Library of Congress Cataloging in Publication Data

Evans, John Martin.
    America—the view from Europe.

    (The Portable Stanford)
    Bibliography
    Includes index.
    1. United States—Civilization.   2.   United States—Foreign opinion, European.   3.   Public opinion—Europe.   I.   Title.
    E169.1.E83   1976b   973   76-40688
    ISBN 0-913374-50-4
    ISBN 0-913374-51-2 pbk.

Simon and Schuster Order Number 22381 (cloth); 22382 (paper)

Trade distribution by Simon and Schuster
A Gulf + Western Company

Printed in the United States of America
10 9 8 7 6 5 4 3 2 1

This book was published originally as part of THE PORTABLE STANFORD, a series of books published by the Stanford Alumni Association, Stanford, California. This edition published by arrangement with the Stanford Alumni Association.

CONTENTS

CREDITS

PAGE ii   Holbein, Ambrosius. *Vtopiae Insvlae Figura*. 1516. Woodcut. Frontispiece of original edition of Sir Thomas More's *Utopia*. From *The Complete Works of Sir Thomas More*. Yale University Press.

PAGE 5   Gudin, Théodore. *Jacques Cartier Discovering the St. Lawrence*. 1847. Oil on canvas. Musée National du Chateau de Versailles, Versailles.

PAGE 9   Anonymous. First printed views of islands found by Christopher Columbus. Woodcut. Published in *Oceanica Classis*, Johann Bergmann de Olpe, Basel, 1493. Used with permission from *How They Saw the New World* by Ernst and Johanna Lehner, © 1966. Tudor Publishing Co., Leon Amiel-Publisher, New York.

PAGE 20   Anonymous, German. *The European Dream; The American Reality*. c. 1830. Aquatint. Bibliothèque Nationale, Paris.

PAGE 28   Browne, Hablôt Knight (Phiz). *The Thriving City of Eden as it appeared on Paper*, illustration to Charles Dickens' *Martin Chuzzlewit*. 1843. Lithograph. From first edition, Cleveland Public Library, Literature Department, Rare Books.

PAGE 30   Browne, Hablôt Knight (Phiz). *The Thriving City of Eden as it appeared in Fact*, illustration to Charles Dickens' *Martin Chuzzlewit*. 1843. Lithograph. Case Western Reserve University, Freiberger Library, Cleveland.

PAGE 36   Blake, Peter. *A Transfer*. 1963. Ink, crayon, and pencil. Collection, Michael White, London. Reprinted with permission from *Pop Art* by John Russell and Suzi Gablik. London: Thames & Hudson, Ltd., 1969.

PAGE 42   Wood, Grant. *Spring Turning*. 1936. Oil on masonite. Private collection.

PAGE 43   From "Mending Wall" in *The Poetry of Robert Frost*, edited by Edward Connery Lathem. Copyright 1930, 1939, © 1969 by Holt, Rinehart and Winston. Copyright © 1958 by Robert Frost. Copyright © 1967 by Lesley Frost Ballantine. Reprinted by permission of Holt, Rinehart and Winston Publishers.

PAGE 45   Hockney, David. *A Bigger Splash*. 1968. Acrylic on canvas. Collection, Lord Dufferin, London. Photograph courtesy of Kasmin Limited, London.

PAGE 48   Stella, Joseph. *New York Interpreted, III: The Skyscrapers*. 1920-22. Oil on canvas. The Newark Museum, Newark.

PAGE 60   Buchser, Frank. *Landscape near Fort Laramie*. 1866. Oil on canvas. Offentliche Kunstmuseum, Basel.

PAGE 73   Still from *Metropolis*. 1926. UFA, sets by Otto Hanke. Photograph courtesy National Film Archive, London.

PAGE 78   Cranach the Elder, Lucas. *Fall of Man*. Oil on canvas. University of London, Courtauld Institute Galleries, Lee Collection.

PAGE 82   Turner, Joseph. *Rain, Steam, Speed*. Oil on canvas. The National Gallery, London.

PAGE 84   Anonymous, German, probably Augsburg or Nuremberg. *The People of the Islands Recently Discovered*. c. 1505. Woodcut with color wash. Bayerisches Staatsbibliothek, Munich.

PAGE 87   Gobelins Tapestry Factory. *Les Nouvelles Indes*. 1737–63. Tapestry. Courtesy Palazzo del Quirinale, Rome.

PAGE 90   Anonymous, after Hans Staden. *Cannibal Scene*. Engraving. From Théodor de Bry, *America, Part III*, 1592. Bibliothèque Nationale, Paris.

PAGE 100   Anonymous. *The Spanish Treatment of Fugitive Black Slaves*. 1595. Engraving. Illustration from Théodor de Bry, *America, Part V*. The British Library, London.

PAGE 104   Van der Street, Jan (called Stradanus). *Vespucci Discovering America*. 1589. Pen and ink. The Metropolitan Museum of Art, New York. Gift of the estate of James Hazen Hyde, 1959.

PAGE 109   Anonymous. *Pocahontas*. c. 1616. Oil on canvas. National Portrait Gallery, Smithsonian Institution, Washington, D.C.

PAGE 118   Delaune, Etienne. *Americca*. 1575. Engraving. The New York Historical Society, New York.

PREFACE

COUNTRIES HAVE A HABIT of becoming metaphors, and America is no exception. Indeed, it has probably stood for more things to more people than any other nation on the face of the globe. This book is about some of the things America has meant to the people of Europe from the Renaissance to the present day. I say "some" advisedly, for a truly comprehensive survey of the way in which the New World has been represented and misrepresented in the literature of the Old would be a lifetime's occupation. The traditional way of reducing the subject to manageable proportions has been to concentrate upon a single national literature or a single historical period. Since there already exist several excellent studies that have followed one or the other of these procedures (see the section on secondary studies in the Reader's Guide), I decided instead to select some of the most enduring themes in European commentary on America and explore their implications with reference to as wide a chronological and geographical range of material as possible.

As it turned out, the six themes I eventually selected grouped themselves into three sets of complementary pairs. Under the heading "American Myths" I have treated the Utopian and anti-Utopian visions of the New World elaborated by such writers as Sir Thomas More, Charles Dickens, and Evelyn Waugh. Under the heading "American Values" I have discussed two interrelated aspects of the emphasis on openness which Vladimir Nabokov and Franz Kafka, among others, have noted in the physical, social, and moral architecture of the United States. And under the heading "American Character" I have examined the way in which the men and women of this country have been portrayed in works like Graham Greene's *The Quiet American* and Henry James' *The Portrait of a Lady*.

My qualifications for dealing with these topics are experiential rather than academic. Having spent the first twenty-eight years of my life in Great Britain, I can personally testify to the power which many of the ideas I shall be describing continue to exercise over the European imagination. Having spent the last thirteen years of my life in America, I feel sufficiently emancipated from those ideas to analyze them with a certain degree of impartiality. Not, however, with complete impartiality. Everyone who writes about America has an axe to grind, and from time to time no doubt I shall take a turn at the whetstone myself. Whenever I do so, my comments will inevitably be colored by the fact that my firsthand acquaintance with the United States has for the most part been confined to California. What is more, the comments of virtually every author I shall be mentioning in the following pages will reflect similar limitations. For the way in which any given European perceives this country will obviously be influenced by a variety of individual factors: where he came from, when he arrived, what he saw, whom he met, and, most important of all perhaps, whether he came as an immigrant or as a visitor. With this consideration in mind I have tried to include enough different writers (over sixty) from enough different countries (Great Britain, France, Germany, Italy, Russia, Spain) in enough different centuries (all five which have elapsed since the discovery) to avoid a merely parochial interpretation of the American scene.

In order to make room for so many points of view I have been forced to omit such classics as Tocqueville's *Democracy in America* and Bryce's *The American Commonwealth*. Since both works are even better known in this country than they are in Europe, I thought it preferable to introduce the reader to some of the less familiar material on the subject—Kafka's *Amerika*, for instance, or Amis' *One Fat Englishman*. I make no apology, on the other hand, for the amount of direct quotation I have permitted myself. If my study was to provide a reasonably accurate account of the images of America which exist in the European mind, it seemed to me essential that wherever possible the images themselves should be presented in their original form, unrefracted by my paraphrase.

As the word "images" implies, my concern throughout this study will be with imaginative constructs rather than historical realities, with the eye of the beholder rather than the countenance of the beheld. "Other people's idea of a man," said Spinoza, "is apt to be a better expression of *their* nature than of *his*," and the same principle applies surely to other people's idea of a country. We reveal our national identities most completely, that is to say, when we are ostensibly describing the peculiar characteristics of another culture. Nowhere is Mark Twain more quintessentially American, for instance, than when he is poking fun at European customs in *The Innocents Abroad*. And by the same token, nowhere is Evelyn Waugh more quintessentially British than when he is satirizing American attitudes in *The Loved One*. In the final analysis, then, the images of America I shall be presenting will have as much to tell us about those who formed them as about those who appear in them. The extent to which they reflect the true nature of American society and character is, to say the least, an open question. This book is an attempt to pose it.

J. Martin Evans

Stanford, California
March 23, 1976

ACKNOWLEDGMENTS

THIS BOOK HAD ITS ORIGINS in a course I taught at the Stanford Overseas Campus in Florence on "The European Image of America" in the summer of 1969 and again in the autumn of 1972. Since then, a research grant from the Committee on International Relations has enabled me to explore the topic in considerably greater detail, and a series of invitations to address various branches of the Stanford Alumni Association has given me an opportunity to subject some of the resultant theories to the test of public discussion. The most recent of these invitations came from the Stanford Women's Club of San Francisco, to whom I delivered the six lectures upon which the present study is based. I would like to thank all those students and alumni who have heard me discuss this subject in one form or another. Their questions and comments have corrected many hasty generalizations and provided many fresh insights. I am also most grateful to my Stanford colleagues Professor George Dekker of the English Department and Professor David Kennedy of the History Department for the time and attention which they generously devoted to reading my original draft, and to Cynthia Fry Gunn, editor of The Portable Stanford, who put in a tremendous amount of work on this book. Their vigilant scrutiny has preserved me from many a stylistic infelicity, factual inaccuracy, and logical discontinuity. Any ill-favored things that remain, to adapt a phrase of Touchstone's, are mine own. Finally, I owe a deep debt of gratitude to my Swiss wife Mariella, my American daughter Jessica, and my British daughter Joanna for bearing with me while I was in the throes of composition. This book is dedicated to them.

CHAPTER ONE

THE BEST OF ALL POSSIBLE WORLDS

Noplacia was once my name,
That is, a place where no one goes.
Plato's Republic now I claim
To match, or beat at its own game;
For that was just a myth in prose,
But what he wrote of, I became,
Of men, wealth, laws a solid frame,
A place where every wise man goes:
Goodplacia is now my name.

> Paul Turner's translation of an anonymous Latin poem included among the prefatory material of the first edition of *Utopia* in 1516

IF WE HEARD that a book had been written by a European statesman describing a country in which the people wear standardized clothes, the towns all look alike, divorce is more common than anywhere else, every form of religious belief is tolerated, the political system consists of an elaborate mechanism of checks and balances designed to ensure the preservation of democracy, strenuous efforts are made to subvert the governments of hostile powers without engaging in all-out war, and it is a long-standing policy to furnish embattled allies with "money abundantly, but citizens very sparingly," most of us would probably infer that the country in question was America. Strictly speaking we would be wrong, for the book I have just summarized (albeit rather selectively) is Sir Thomas More's *Utopia*, and the country it describes is a fictional island located somewhere in the South Atlantic. But in broader terms we would be right, for as the contemporary historian A.L. Rowse has put it, "*Utopia* is the first, and a most distinguished, reflection of the New World in the literature of the Old." Indeed, More's visionary work defines more accurately than many subsequent accounts the promise that America has held out to Europe from the sixteenth century to the present.

An Ideal Commonwealth

"Since it has been my intention to write something which may be of use to the understanding reader," declared Niccolò Machiavelli in a famous chapter of *The Prince* (1513), "it has seemed wiser to me to follow the real truth of the matter rather than what we imagine it to be. For imagination has created many principalities and republics that have never been seen or known to have any real existence, for how we live is so different from how we ought to live that he who studies what ought to be done rather than what is done will learn the way to his downfall rather than to his preservation." He produced accordingly a manual of political maneuvers in which he instructed Lorenzo de' Medici how to remain in power by exploiting the corruption and vice of his fellow men. Yet only two years after Machiavelli penned those words an equally tough-minded and realistic politician, Sir Thomas More, created in his *Utopia* what the introduction to the first edition claimed was "an ideal commonwealth, a pattern and finished model of conduct, than which there has never been seen in the world one more wholesome in its institutions, or more perfect, or to be thought more desirable." If this description of the work was even remotely accurate, the future Chancellor of England had evidently decided that he could be "of use to the understanding reader" by putting into his hands not a cynical introduction to the game of power politics but an idealistic model of the well-governed state.

More's decision can be explained, I believe, by three crucial events, one historical and two literary. The historical event, of course, was the discovery of the New World in 1492. The literary events were the publication in 1505 of Amerigo Vespucci's account of his four voyages to America and in 1511 of Peter Martyr's narrative of Columbus' exploits in Hispaniola (the modern Haiti) and Cuba. So far as I have been able to discover, there is no evidence that Machiavelli was at all interested in, or even knew very much about, the momentous discoveries that were being made across the Atlantic while he was in the service of the Florentine Republic. More, on the contrary, was closely acquainted with the voyages of discovery, and in more ways than one. Not only had he read Vespucci's pamphlets and Martyr's *The New World* with considerable attention; he was also related by marriage to the English explorer John Rastell, whose ill-fated expedition to America took place just a year after *Utopia* was published. As we shall see, it was this literary and personal interest in the exploration of the New World that fostered More's Utopian vision and shaped many of its most characteristic features.

The New World

What gave the discovery of America its extraordinary importance in the eyes of sixteenth-century Europeans was a fact which, had he known it, might have led Machiavelli to temper his skepticism concerning the possibility of achieving an ideal society in the real world. For according to Vespucci and Martyr, not to mention Columbus himself, recent explorations in the West had revealed not just a new world but a golden one in which humanity lived in a state of unfallen innocence such as Adam and Eve had originally possessed in the garden of Eden. "They go naked," Martyr wrote of the inhabitants of Hispaniola, "and they know neither weights nor measures, nor that source of all misfortunes, money; living in a golden age, without laws, without lying judges, without books, satisfied with their life, and in no wise solicitous for the future." If reports such as these were to be believed, there already existed in the New World the kind of ideal society which the author of *The Prince* claimed had never been "known to have any real existence." The gap between what Machiavelli called "the real truth of the matter" as opposed to "what we imagine it to be" had been narrowed if not abolished altogether. Fact in this instance had turned out to be as edifying as fiction was expected to be, and the human imagination was free to dream of "what ought to be done" without being accused of indulging in mere wish-fulfillment fantasies. For a time, at least, the discoveries across the Atlantic blurred the traditional distinction between the imaginary and the actual, the fictional and the historical. As late as 1589 it was thus possible for Edmund Spenser, the author of perhaps the most unrealistic narrative poem in the English language, to defend the credibility of *The Faerie Queene* by reminding his readers:

> That of the world least part to us is read [revealed];
> And daily how through hardy enterprise
> Many great regions are discovered,

Which to late age were never mentioned.
Who ever heard of th'Indian Peru?
Or who in venturous vessel measured
The Amazon's huge river, now found true?
Or fruitfullest Virginia, who did ever view?

Yet all these were, when no man did them know
Yet have from wisest ages hidden been;
And later times things more unknown shall show.
Why then should witless man so much misween [misconceive]
That nothing is but that which he hath seen?

No longer was the mind of Europe imprisoned within the corrupt and depressing world which Machiavelli had so memorably portrayed in *The Prince*. Spenser's Fairyland could be as real as Lorenzo de' Medici's Florence.

The Golden Age

The immediate effect of Columbus' exploits, then, was to liberate the European imagination from the gloomy confines of its recent history, with the result that the idealistic impulse, which in the Middle Ages had been directed largely to the next world, could now be focused upon this one. Adam and Eve were alive and well and living in the terrestrial paradise on the other side of the Atlantic. Far from being a long-lost period in the distant past of the human race, the Golden Age was still flourishing in Renaissance America. It is no accident, therefore, that the passage from Martyr's *New World* that I quoted earlier sounds very much like a recollection of the Roman poet Ovid's description of the Age of Gold in Book I of his *Metamorphoses*:

> In the beginning was the Golden Age when men of their own accord, without the threat of punishment, without laws, maintained good faith and did what was right. There were no penalties to be afraid of . . . indeed there were no judges, men lived securely without them. . . . The peoples of the world, untroubled by any fears, enjoyed a leisurely and peaceful existence, and had no use for soldiers. The earth itself, without compulsion, untouched by the hoe, produced all things spontaneously, and men were content with foods that grew without cultivation.

Over and over again in the travel literature of the Renaissance one can hear Ovid's phrases being echoed in the accounts of the New World. Here, for instance, is a paragraph from Montaigne's essay "On Cannibals" (1579-80):

Jacques Cartier Discovering the St. Lawrence by Théodore Gudin.

To my apprehension, what we now see in those natives does not only surpass all the images with which the poets have adorned the golden age, and all their inventions in feigning a happy state of man, but moreover the fancy, and even the wish and desire of philosophy itself. . . . Should I tell Plato that it is a nation wherein there is no manner of traffic, no knowledge of letters, no science of numbers, no name of magistrate, no political superiority; no use of service, riches or poverty; no contracts, no successions, no dividends, no properties, no employments but those of leisure; no respect of kindred, but in common; no clothing, no agriculture, no metal, no use of corn or wine; . . . how much would he find his imaginary republic short of this perfection?

Thirty years later Shakespeare was to remember this description, which he had read in John Florio's English translation of 1603, and incorporate it into the musings of the honest old counselor Gonzalo in *The Tempest* (1611-12):

Had I plantation of this isle . . . no kind of traffic
Would I admit; no name of magistrate;
Letters should not be known; riches, poverty,
And use of service, none; contract, succession,
Bourn, bound of land, tilth, vineyard, none;
No use of metal, corn, or wine, or oil;
No occupation; all men idle, all;
And women too, but innocent and pure;
No sovereignty. . . .
All things in common nature should produce
Without sweat or endeavour. Treason, felony,
Sword, pike, knife, gun, or need of any engine,
Would I not have; but nature should bring forth,
Of its own kind, all foison, all abundance,
To feed my innocent people. . . .
I would with such perfection govern, sir,
T'excel the golden age.

By the time Shakespeare wrote this speech, however, almost exactly a hundred years had passed since Martyr had resurrected Ovid's vision of the Golden Age, and the vision had begun to tarnish. As a result, what in Martyr's *New World* and Montaigne's "On Cannibals" had purported to be an accurate description of life across the Atlantic is now just an old man's dream punctuated by the cynical asides of his companions. "Prithee, no more," commands Alonso, the ruler of a real state, at the end of Gonzalo's speech, "thou dost talk nothing to me."

Fact and Fiction

When More was writing his *Utopia*, on the other hand, the concept of the Golden Age had not yet lapsed back into the world of fantasy from which Martyr had originally drawn it. For the men and women of the early sixteenth century who had read Vespucci's *Four Voyages* or Martyr's *New World*, the ideal state was a contemporary reality. By locating his imaginary island in the historical and geographical milieu of the explorers, More could thus give his story the kind of inherent plausibility that the first landing on the moon conferred upon much of our modern science fiction. And this, of course, is precisely what he did, with the result that Utopia is so deeply embedded in circumstantial detail that it is often difficult to tell at what point the facts end and the fiction begins.

The island is described, to begin with, by Raphael Hythloday, a fictional sailor who, we learn in the opening pages of the book, accompanied the factual Amerigo Vespucci on the last three of his four voyages. Indeed, it was during the fourth voyage that he came across Utopia, for Hythloday "did not return home with [Vespucci] on the last voyage. After much effort, he won permission from Americus to be one of the twenty-four who were left in a fort at the farthest place at which they touched in their last voyage." The reference here is to Vespucci's own account of his four voyages, which, as More accurately informs us, had recently been published. "After sailing for two hundred and sixty leagues," Vespucci had written, "we entered a harbor where we determined to build an outpost. Having done so, we left behind in this fort twenty-four Christians who had been the crew of the ship of our commander in chief. . . . We left in the fort the twenty-four Christians, giving them twelve guns and many more arms, and supplying them with provisions to last them six months."

It was from this base, Hythloday goes on to explain in *Utopia*, that he explored other islands in the New World, among them the realm of King Utopus. Picking up the story where the *Four Voyages* left off, "[Hythloday] told us that when Vespucius had sailed away, he and his companions that had stayed behind in the fort often met the people of the country, and by fair and gentle speech gradually won their favor. Before long they came to dwell with them quite safely and even familiarly. He also told us that they were esteemed by the prince (I have forgotten his name and his country), who furnished them plentifully with all things necessary, and who also gave them the means of traveling, both boats when they went by water and wagons when they went by land." From the very outset, More's legendary island is thus securely anchored in the historical and geographical realities of the age of exploration. To a sixteenth-century reader familiar with those realities, *Utopia* must have seemed as credible as a tale purporting to come from one of Neil Armstrong's fellow astronauts would seem to us today.

Perhaps the best example of More's reliance on the documented experiences of the discoverers has to do with the feature of Utopian life that his contemporaries might otherwise have regarded as most far-fetched, namely the absence of private property. For according to both Columbus and Vespucci, the social system that Plato had advocated in his *Republic* was actually being practiced by the inhabitants of the New World. "It is proven," wrote Martyr, "that amongst them the land belongs to everybody, just as does the sun or the water. They know no difference between *meum* and *tuum* [mine and yours], that source of all evils. . . . It is indeed a golden age, neither ditches nor hedges, nor walls enclose their domains; they live in gardens open to all, without laws, without judges." And in an equally famous passage, Vespucci declared in his letter to Lorenzo de' Medici, first published in 1503 under the title *The New World*, "The inhabitants of the New World do not have goods of their own, but all things are held in common. They live together without king, without government, and each is his own master. . . . They live according to nature, and may be called Epicureans rather than Stoics. . . . There is a great abundance of gold, and by them it is in no respect esteemed or valued. . . . And surely if the terrestrial paradise be in any part of this earth, I esteem that it is not far distant from these parts." Here, clearly enough, is the source of More's insistence that in Utopia all things are held in common and every form of personal wealth is despised. Far from being a mere flight of fancy, the communism of More's *Utopia* was one of its most realistic elements.

• The Utopian System

There is, however, another and still more fundamental sense in which *Utopia* may be called a realistic work, far more realistic than Gonzalo's idealistic daydream in *The Tempest*, for example, or any of the legends of the Golden Age that lie behind it. For unlike so many other authors who have proposed a model of the ideal state, More did not take the intrinsic perfection of its inhabitants as a given. As a matter of fact, the view of human nature expounded in *Utopia* has rather more in common with Machiavelli's than with Gonzalo's. "All those who have written upon civil institutions," asserted the former in his *Discourses* (1512-?), "demonstrate that whoever desires to found a state and give it

The first printed views of the new islands found by Christopher Columbus.
(From Columbus' letter, published in *Oceanica Classis*.)

laws, must start with assuming that all men are bad and ever ready to display their vicious nature whenever they may find occasion for it." *Utopia*, it seems to me, is grounded on precisely the same assumption. Book I, after all, is little more than a grim catalogue of the ills and injustices of sixteenth-century Europe in which the realities of Renaissance power politics are analyzed in terms every bit as disenchanting as those in *The Prince*. "It is impossible to do all things well," More observes glumly at one point of the discussion, "unless all men are good, and this I do not expect to see for a long time." And Hythloday, the discoverer of Utopia, is equally skeptical about the likelihood of persuading his fellow men to behave less viciously than they have in the past. "Seeing that men will not fit their ways to Christ's pattern," he remarks scornfully, "the preachers have fitted his teaching to human customs, to get agreement somehow or other. The only result I can see is that men become more confirmed in their wickedness."

Thus the question inevitably arises: how could either Hythloday or More possibly square the existence of an ideal state like Utopia, where all things do appear to be done well, with their belief in the inherent depravity of the human race? The answer is: quite easily. For when we examine the various political and social institutions of Utopia, it quickly becomes apparent that they are not predicated on the perfection of the citizens for whom they were designed. On the contrary, King Utopus seems to have consistently assumed the worst about his subjects when he framed the laws that govern them. For instance, there are ingenious safeguards built into the political system to ensure that "the prince and the tranibors may not conspire together to change the government and enslave the people." The senate never debates an issue on the day it is introduced but defers the question to the next meeting "so that a man will not let his tongue run away with him and then strive to defend his foolish first thoughts instead of considering the public good. They know that through a perverse and preposterous pride a man may prefer to sacrifice the common good to his own hasty opinions for fear of being thought heedless and shortsighted." In the domestic realm the laws imply an equally cynical view of those whose behavior they were framed to regulate. Extramarital affairs are severely punished on the grounds that "few would unite in married love, to spend their whole lives with one person and put up with all the annoyances of marriage, unless they were rigorously restrained from promiscuity." In the military sphere any propensity to cowardice is dealt with by placing the fainthearted "on fortifications where there is no chance of flight" with the result that "they often show themselves brave from sheer necessity." In the economic area full production is ensured by a group of overseers whose only business "is to see that no one sits around in idleness, and that everyone works hard at his trade." And whatever form of religious belief they may have chosen to embrace, the citizens of Utopia are required to acknowledge the existence of an afterlife in which the virtuous will be rewarded and the wicked punished, for "who can doubt that a man who fears nothing but the law and apprehends nothing after death would secretly flout his country's laws or break them by force to satisfy his greed?"

Obviously, then, the inhabitants of Utopia are quite as ambitious, stubborn, lecherous, cowardly, lazy, and greedy as their European contemporaries. Like the men in Machiavelli's *Discourses*, they are "ever ready to display their vicious nature whenever they may find occasion for it." The only difference is that the Utopian constitution does not offer them that occasion, for it is a mechanism designed to eliminate virtually every opportunity for human depravity to express itself. The poor islanders can't be wicked even if they want to be, and the ferocious laws suggest that they want to be fairly often.

In this respect it is interesting to compare More's ideal state with another Renaissance Utopia conceived by a British statesman, Sir Francis Bacon's unfinished fantasy *The New Atlantis* (1626). Written at least partly in response to More's work, it portrays a society of moral paragons somewhere in the South Seas. "You shall understand," a European visitor is informed upon his arrival, "that there is not under the heavens so chaste a nation as this, nor so free from all pollution of foulness. It is the virgin of the world. . . . For there is nothing amongst mortal men more fair and admirable than the chaste minds of this people. Know therefore that with them there are no stews [brothels], no dissolute houses, no courtesans, nor anything of that kind. Nay, they wonder with detestation at you in Europe, which permit such things." There is no sexual misbehavior in Utopia either, but for a very different reason: "No loafing is tolerated, and there are no pretexts for laziness or opportunities. There are no taverns or ale houses, no brothels, no chances for corruption, no hiding places, no secret meetings. Because they live in full view of all, they must do their accustomed labor and spend their leisure honorably." In the New Atlantis there are no brothels because the people are chaste. In Utopia the people are chaste because there are no brothels. Like all the other virtues they exemplify, the Utopians' chastity is the product of the political and social system under which they live rather than the outcome of their own characters. The rationality of More's imaginary state resides not in the governed but in the government, not in the inhabitants but in the system.

This is the crucial difference between Utopia and the descriptions of the Golden Age I quoted earlier. As we saw, Ovid had characterized that period in the history of mankind by the absence of both laws and judges while Montaigne, taking his cue from Martyr, had asserted that the so-called barbarians discovered by Columbus and Vespucci had no word for magistrate and no legal contracts. More's Utopia, in contrast, is a quintessentially legalistic construction, a tissue of rules and regulations which simply could not operate without strict judicial enforcement. As a hardheaded political realist as well as a devout Catholic, More clearly found it inconceivable that in a post-lapsarian world the descendants of Adam and Eve were capable of spontaneous and continuous virtue. For him the New World represented not so much a second garden of Eden as a chance to remedy some of the consequences of man's Fall in the first.

It was this distinction that I had in mind when I claimed earlier that *Utopia* defines more accurately than many subsequent works the promise which America, since the time of its discovery, has held out to Europe. For Hythloday's major thesis is not that the imperfections of the human race can be miraculously erased by the mere act of crossing the Atlantic. It is simply that those imperfections could be controlled and minimized by a set of social and political institutions that do not permit our innate sinfulness as much scope as it has found in the Old World. Both people and things, he believes, can be made to work if not perfectly at least better. The claim that he makes for Utopia is only that it is the best of all *possible* worlds.

Citizens of the World

More's refusal to idealize the inhabitants of his Utopia may well explain why they do not feel compelled, as so many of their successors did, to isolate themselves from the rest of the international community. A society of saints might well run the risk of moral contamination if it exposed itself to the outside world, but a society whose strength lies in its system of government rather than in the character of its citizens has nothing to fear from contact with its less enlightened neighbors. Again, the contrast with Bacon's *New Atlantis* is instructive. In the land of the Bensalemites, as they are called, travel abroad is forbidden to all except a few trusted members of the inner circle, and visitors are not admitted unless they are in desperate need of provisions. As a result, declares the governor with evident satisfaction, his country has succeeded in avoiding "novelties and commixture of manners." The Utopians, on the contrary, are eager not only to admit any "novelties" that may be of use to them but also to share their own culture with the rest of mankind. "Ungrudgingly do I share my benefits with others," announces the Utopian poem that More quotes at the beginning of the book, "undemurringly do I adopt whatever is better from others."

In accordance with the first part of this policy, the government of Utopia has regular diplomatic relations with other states, however benighted the latter might be, and on at least one occasion has persuaded them to accept its own system of values. In one of the book's best-known episodes the Anemolian ambassadors, who have made the mistake of arriving in the Utopian capital "decked out with all those things which among the Utopians were considered badges of slavery, signs of punishment, or toys for children," are greeted with such hilarity that they quickly learn to treat gold and jewels with the same contempt as their hosts do. Nor is moral enlightenment the only benefit that the inhabitants of More's ideal commonwealth are willing to share with their neighbors. They are also willing to provide military assistance when the need arises. Although they prefer not to make formal treaties of alliance, Hythloday points out, the Utopians have more than once gone to war to protect the territory "of their friends if an enemy has invaded it, or to free some wretched people from tyrannous oppression and servitude."

They are equally ready, moreover, to receive assistance, whether material or intellectual. Their delight in learning, declares Hythloday at the end of Book I, "is the real reason for their being better governed and for their living more happily than we do," and in Book II he illustrates his point with two particularly striking examples: the eagerness with which the Utopians undertook the study of Greek (so that they could read the classical texts he had brought them) and the speed with which they learned to manufacture paper and construct a printing press (so that they could reproduce the texts they found most valuable). But the most remarkable example of all occurs in Hythloday's account of the Utopians' response to what for them was a completely alien religion: "We told them," he relates, "of the name, doctrine, manner of life, and miracles of Christ, and of the wonderful constancy of the many martyrs. ... You will hardly believe with what favorably disposed minds they received this account . . . , many came over to our religion and were baptized."

Here again More was very probably drawing upon the experience of the early explorers, who frequently remarked upon the willingness of the inhabitants of the New World to assimilate the manners and religion of the Old. Whatever its source, his observation has been repeated over and over again in European descriptions of America from the sixteenth century to the present. For despite its physical isolation, America has always been noted for its astonishing openness to foreign

novelties whether culinary, artistic, technical, institutional, or ideo-
logical. Perhaps the most obvious expression of this readiness to "adopt
whatever is better from others," as the Utopian poem put it, is the
aura that the word "imported" has in the United States (in Britain the
only adjective of comparable selling power, until recently at least, was
"British-made"), but one might also cite the numerous "perfect replicas"
of European buildings described in such works as Evelyn Waugh's *The
Loved One* (1948) and Paul Bourget's charming essay *Outre-Mer, Impressions of America* (1895). "One of [the wealthy residents of New-
port]," writes the latter:

> has spent some time in England, and it has pleased him to
> build for himself on one of these Rhode Island lawns an En-
> glish abbey of the style of Queen Elizabeth. It rises up, gray
> and stern, so like, so perfect, that it might, without changing a
> single stone, be transported to Oxford on the shores of Isis,
> to make a pendant to the delicious cloister of Magdalen or the
> facade of Oriel. Another man loves France, and he has seen
> fit to possess in sight of the Atlantic a chateau in the style of
> the French Renascence. Here is the chateau; it reminds you
> of Azay, Chenonceaux, and the Loire, with its transparent
> ribbon of water winding idly in and out amid the yellow sand
> of the islands. A third has built a marble palace precisely like
> the Trianon, with Corinthian pillars as large as those of the
> Temple of the Sun at Baalbek. And these are not weak imita-
> tions, pretentious and futile attempts, such as in every country
> bring ridicule upon braggarts and upstarts. No. In detail and
> finish they reveal conscientious study, technical care.

To a European eye the same impulse is recognizable in virtually every
facet of American culture—from the incorporation into the constitu-
tional plans for Pennsylvania, Carolina, and New Jersey of features
which William Penn had admired in the government of Venice, to the
transplantation of French vine stocks to the valleys of California. The
land developer who recently transported London Bridge to the middle
of the Arizona desert was simply carrying on what Paul Bourget has
suggested is a long-standing American tradition, "the constant, tireless
endeavor to absorb European ideas."

According to the British anthropologist Geoffrey Gorer, indeed, the
American genius finds its most complete expression in assimilation and
adaptation rather than in creation or invention. Just as the Utopians
"made themselves masters of all our useful inventions" by applying
and extending the principles they learned from such European visitors

as Hythloday, so, Gorer argues in *The American People* (1948), the United States first acquired the foreign products she wished to reproduce, in this case rocket weapons, "then she imported the craftsmen, the German scientists, and analyzed their behavior; and then, when these analyses had been completed, she set about producing bigger and better rockets, capable of going higher and farther than the German originals." For Gorer this process is a model of the relationship between American and European culture. Intellectually, if not physically, the United States is still perceived in Europe as "a citizen of the world," to borrow a phrase from Bacon's essay *Of Goodness and Goodness of Nature* (1625), "no island cut off from other lands but a continent that joins to them."

Separate but Superior

As the general direction of the cultural traffic I have just been describing may suggest, the New World has always seemed far more willing to learn than the Old—and not because it stands in greater need of instruction either. The plain fact is that Europe has been almost as resistant to foreign influences as America has been open to them. It may from time to time admit a new vegetable (the potato), a new vice (smoking), or a new disease (syphilis), but it has rarely entertained the prospect of "Americanization" with anything but profound repugnance. Despite the Utopians' readiness to share their benefits with others, Hythloday is thus extremely doubtful whether his fellow Europeans will be disposed to accept them. After pointing out how much intellectual profit the Utopians had derived early in their history from a group of Romans who had been shipwrecked on their shores, he observes wryly that "if a similar accident has hitherto brought any men here from their land, it has been completely forgotten, as doubtless it will be forgotten in time to come that I was ever in their country." Indeed, his whole account of Utopia is predicated on the assumption that Europe is too old, too fixed in its ways, to learn anything from the ideal commonwealth across the Atlantic, and many modern commentators would agree with him. In works as diverse as George Santayana's *Character and Opinion in the United States* (1920) and Jean-François Revel's *Without Marx or Jesus* (1970), one encounters the same basic theme: Europe is a lost cause, the prisoner of its own appalling history. Whereas America "is in the process of evolution," writes Revel, Europe "is culturally stagnant." European history, he concludes, "is only repeating itself; or, more accurately, it has been reduced to quibbling."

In the "Old and rotting World," as Humbert Humbert calls it in Nabokov's *Lolita* (1955), the burden of the past consequently appears to be too great to permit anything but the kind of minor modifications and adjustments that More proposes in Book I of *Utopia*. Even if one can't revolutionize the ancient system, More argues, one can at least try to patch it up here and there: "If evil opinions cannot be quite rooted out, and if you cannot correct habitual attitudes as you wish, you must not therefore abandon the commonwealth. Don't give up the ship in a storm because you cannot control the winds. And do not force unheard-of advice upon people, when you know that their minds are different from yours. You must strive to guide policy indirectly, so that you make the best of things, and what you cannot turn to good, you can at least make less bad." Here speaks the authentic voice of European empiricism, the voice we heard at the beginning of this chapter in Machiavelli's sober insistence on confining one's attention to the real truth of the matter and not bothering one's head with Utopian speculations which can never be translated into practice. But the visionary Hythloday will have nothing to do with any form of compromise. "A man has no chance to do good when his colleagues are more likely to corrupt the best of men than be corrected by them," he replies. "He will either be corrupted himself by his colleagues, or, if he remains sound and innocent, he will be blamed for the folly and knavery of others. He is far from being able to mend matters by guiding policy indirectly." And in any case, Hythloday continues, mere tinkering with the social and political mechanism is no longer enough. What Europe needs is nothing less than a completely fresh start, a chance to build a new and better society in a land uncluttered by the sins and follies of the past.

This, as we have seen, is precisely the chance which More and his contemporaries believed the discovery of America had provided. By the mere act of locating his ideal state on the other side of the Atlantic, the author of *Utopia* was thus giving concrete expression to a belief that has never lost its hold over the European imagination, the belief that, in Revel's words, "America offers the only possible escape for mankind." Small wonder, then, if Europeans seem to get so much angrier with this country than they do with any other. For in the final analysis they criticize America with such vehemence not, I think, because they resent its wealth or its power but rather because they have always projected upon the New World their faith in the capacity of the human race to create a Utopia. No country in the history of Western civilization has had to bear as great a weight of idealism as this. So when England or France or Germany commits some national outrage, it can be treated by the other members of the European family as just another sign of the inveterate weakness of a tiresome relative—that's the English for you; how typically French; just like the Germans, etc. But when the nation which the French commentator R.L. Bruckberger describes as "the best hope on earth for the West" falls short of European expectations, it feels like a betrayal rather than a mere failure. As another French writer, Simone de Beauvoir points out, what happens in America simply seems to matter more. "That is what moved me most strongly when I took my leave," she writes in the final paragraph of *America Day by Day* (1947). "America is a pivotal point in the world where the future of man is at stake. To like America or not to like her; these words have no sense. Here is a battlefield, and one can only follow with excitement the struggle she carries on within herself, the stakes of which are beyond measure."

Postscript: The Impossible Dream

Unlike his American alter ego Raphael Hythloday and his European brother-in-law John Rastell, Sir Thomas More chose to remain in the Old World and to follow there the advice he gave Hythloday in Book I of *Utopia*, not "to abandon the commonwealth" but rather to "strive to guide policy indirectly." As Lord Chancellor of England More did in fact attempt to persuade Henry VIII to act less foolishly and wickedly. But in the end it was Hythloday who had the last word, for as he had prophesied, in a corrupt court the man of principle was "blamed for the folly and knavery of others": More's attempt to "guide policy indirectly" cost him his life.

In the New World, however, it was a rather different story. There it was Hythloday who proved to be too optimistic. For although *Utopia* had a profound influence on the earliest attempts to settle both South and North America (Vasco de Quiroga drew up a scheme in 1530 for creating a Utopian society in Santa Fe, and the leader of the first English colonial expedition, Sir Humfrey Gilbert, took a copy of More's work along with him in 1583), every experiment in common ownership ended in failure. According to Captain John Smith, for instance, the turning point in the history of Virginia came when the governor decided to abandon the Utopian system in favor of private property. "When our people were fed out of the common store," he recounted in his *General History of Virginia* (1624), "and labored jointly together, glad was he that could slip from his labor or slumber over his task, he cared not how; nay, the most honest among them would hardly take so much true pains in a week as now for themselves they will do in a day; neither cared they for the increase, presuming that howsoever the harvest prospered, the general store must maintain them, so that we reaped not so much corn from the labors of thirty as now three or four do provide for themselves." William Bradford describes a similar experience in his great *History of Plymouth Plantation* (1650):

> At length, after much debate of things, the Governor (with advice of the chiefest among them) gave way that they should set corn every man for his own particular, and in that regard trust to themselves. . . . And so assigned to every family a parcel of land, according to the proportion of their number for that end. . . . This had very good success; for it made all hands very industrious, so as much more corn was planted than otherwise would have been by any means the Governor or any other could use, and saved him a great deal of trouble, and gave far better content. The women now went willingly into the field and took their little ones with them to set corn, which before would allege weakness and inability; whom to have compelled would have been thought great tyranny and oppression. The experience that was had in this common course and condition, tried sundry years, and that amongst godly and sober men, may well evince the vanity of that conceit of Plato's and other ancients, applauded by some of later times, that taking away of property and bringing in community into a commonwealth would make them happy and flourishing; as if they were wiser than God.

But perhaps the most telling commentary on *Utopia* was provided not by a colonial administrator but by a Renaissance playwright, George Chapman, who in his play *Eastward Ho* (1605) gave the following speech to a sea captain reporting to some of his cronies on the wonders of the New World: "I tell thee, gold is more plentiful there than copper is with us, and for as much red copper as I can bring I'll have thrice the weight in gold. Why man, all their dripping pans and their chamber pots are pure gold, and all the chains with which they chain up their streets are massy gold. All the prisoners they take are fettered in gold. And for rubies and diamonds, they go forth on holidays and gather them by the sea shore to hang on their children's coats and stick in their caps, as commonly as our children wear saffron gilt brooches and groats with holes in them." This account clearly derives from Hythloday's description of the contempt with which the Utopians treat worldly riches: "While their eating and drinking utensils are made of china and glass," he informs his companions, "beautiful but expensive, their chamber pots and stools both in their public halls and their homes are made of gold and silver. They also use these metals for the chains and fetters of their bondmen. They hang gold rings from the ears of criminals. . . ." But although Chapman's sea captain uses almost the same words, his point is very different. He is suggesting not that his friends should imitate the Americans' contempt for gold but rather that they should exploit it. By a cruel if inevitable irony, what in Utopia had been an attack upon the absurd value put upon these essentially useless metals and minerals by Western Europe has become in the Jacobean play an incentive for crossing the Atlantic in search of them. In less than a century, human cupidity has transformed a critique of European gold fever into a provocation to it.

More himself, I suspect, would not have been too surprised by the fate of Hythloday's ideals. Indeed, during the course of their debate in Book I, he had anticipated many of the arguments that were subsequently brought to bear upon the communist system. In reply to Hythloday's categoric assertion that "so long as private property remains, there is no hope at all that [social ills] may be healed," More contends that "on the contrary . . . it seems to me that men cannot live well where all things are in common. How can there be plenty where every man stops working? The hope of gain will not drive him; and he will rely on others and become lazy." And in spite of Hythloday's insistence that the inhabitants of Utopia are never permitted to indulge in any wasteful or slothful activities, More still comments skeptically at the end of Book II that there are "many things in the Utopian commonwealth which I wish rather than expect to see followed among our citizens."

This mixture of wishing and doubting, aspiration and cynicism, is embodied in the very names that More gave both to his imaginary state and to its discoverer. For as the poem I quoted at the beginning of this chapter reveals, Utopia, in Greek, means both good place (*eu-topos*) and no place (*ou-topos*). And Raphael Hythloday, the first embodiment in European literature of the distinctively American spirit, has an equally ambiguous name. His first name, Raphael, means, in Hebrew, "God has healed"; it was the angel Raphael who traditionally undertook God's missions of mercy. His surname, Hythloday, on the other hand, is of Greek derivation, and means, literally, "dispenser of nonsense." The character whom More invented to articulate the American dream is thus a merciful guide who expounds absurdities, a benevolent windbag who found the good place no place.

The European Dream; The American Reality, anonymous, German.

CHAPTER TWO

A FOOL'S PARADISE

Thus she brought us to the deep-flowing River of Ocean and the
frontiers of the world, where the fog-bound Cimmerians live
in the City of Perpetual Mist. When the bright Sun climbs the sky
and puts the stars to flight, no ray from him can penetrate to them,
nor can he see them as he drops from heaven and sinks once more
to earth. For dreadful Night has spread her mantle over the heads
of that unhappy folk.

      Homer's description of the approaches to the kingdom of the dead in
      The Odyssey, Book XI, translated by E.V. Rieu

"THE EXISTENCE OF AMERICA," wrote C.S. Lewis in his survey of sixteenth-century English literature, "was one of the greatest disappointments in the history of Europe." And so in a sense it was, for Columbus,
Vespucci, and most of the early English explorers had hoped to discover
not a New World but an alternative sea route to the farthest reaches
of the Old, that is, to China or, to give it its Renaissance name, Cathay.
The existence of a large land mass blocking the way was a considerable
inconvenience, and initially at least as much energy was devoted to
finding a way around or through it as to exploring it. Seen from the
short-term economic point of view, America was an obstacle rather
than an opportunity.

Thanks to his extraordinary capacity for self-deception, however, Columbus himself was spared this disappointment. As his various biographers have demonstrated, he refused right up to the end of his life to believe that the new lands he had discovered were anything other than a part of the Indies, as he persisted in calling them. For by overestimating the size of Eurasia by approximately ninety percent and underestimating the size of the globe by approximately twenty-five percent, he had convinced himself that the coast of Japan or Cipangu, as it was known, was only some two thousand four hundred nautical miles from the Canaries, whereas in fact it is ten thousand six hundred. If his calculations were right, Columbus reasoned, it was inconceivable that he had arrived anywhere but Asia, and when the natives of Cuba informed him that there was gold to be found in Cubanacan, which means central Cuba, he thought they must be referring to El Gran Khan, the legendary ruler of Cathay. Cuba, he decided, was the Chinese province of Mangi, and Haiti was either Cipangu itself or part of an archipelago just to the east of it. As the modern historian Edmundo O'Gorman notes in his absorbing study *The Invention of America* (1961), the "coarseness and nudity of the natives, the absence of the great cities and gilded palaces that he expected to find, the fact that gold was only to be heard of in the fallacious words of the Indians, and the repeated failure of his attempts to locate Cipangu and later to establish contact with the Great Khan did nothing to shake his faith: he had reached Asia, he was in Asia, and it was from Asia that he returned. No one, nothing, to the day of his death ever made him relinquish this cherished conviction."

From the moment of its discovery, then, America has been, sometimes quite literally, the creation of European wishful thinking. Only very reluctantly, in the face of mounting evidence, did Columbus' successors accept the existence of a massive continent separating Europe from the fabled riches of the East. After the jubilation generated by the Admiral's mistaken theories about what he had found, there consequently succeeded the profound sense of disappointment to which C.S. Lewis was referring in the statement I quoted earlier. As the New World came to be recognized for what it really was, the optimistic fantasies of the 1490s and early 1500s slowly disappeared in the mists of the Atlantic. America was not what it had appeared to be after all.

Never-Never Land

The same basic pattern of unrealistic expectations followed by bitter disillusionment recurs over and over again in the records of European perceptions of America. Indeed, taken together, the experience of Columbus and those who came immediately after him might serve as a paradigm for almost every encounter between the Old World and the New that has taken place ever since. Throughout its history, one could say without too much exaggeration, America has been taken for something that it isn't (Asia, the ideal state, the terrestrial paradise, to name only the most obvious) and then accused of fraud when its true nature has finally emerged. The sheer weight of idealism which the New World has been forced to bear from the fifteenth century to the twentieth has virtually ensured that one of the keynotes in European writings about it should be disenchantment.

The cycle I have just been describing in the Spanish response to Columbus' discoveries was repeated, for example, by the British in their encounters with the New World almost a century later. Not that the Elizabethan explorers believed that the continent across the Atlantic was Asia. They simply thought that the new territories were going to be a source of instant wealth and prosperity. The riches of America, they convinced themselves and their backers, were there for the taking. All that was required was a nation with the strength of will to seek them out. The best known of this later generation of voyagers is probably Sir Walter Raleigh, who declared that he was inspired by his sovereign "to seek new worlds for gold, for praise, for glory." On his ill-fated voyage up the Orinoco in 1617 he found none of the first and precious little of the other two.

But Raleigh was only one of a long line of British seamen to be deluded by the vision of trans-Atlantic treasure trove. In 1576, almost forty years before his famous quest for the "metal of India," as Sir Toby Belch describes it in Shakespeare's *Twelfth Night* (1599-1600), Sir Martin Frobisher announced that he had found gold on Baffin Island, and on the basis of his claims a brief nautical gold rush developed. Unfortunately for Frobisher, however, the so-called "gold ore" brought back by the expeditions of 1577 and 1578 turned out to be iron pyrites, with the result that, in the words of historian David Quinn, "the first big investment in America was a total disaster for subscribers."

The dreams of another sixteenth-century British fortune hunter, Sir Humfrey Gilbert, proved to be equally fragile. Empowered by the Queen to take possession of any uninhabited lands he could find in the New World, he attempted to cross the Atlantic in 1578, but none of his ships succeeded in making the crossing. Undeterred by this setback, he then proceeded to build what Quinn calls "a paper dominion in America in the next few years, selling lands not yet seen to Catholic gentlemen anxious to avoid increasing taxation, to younger sons of nobles, and the gentry at large, and offering trading privileges to towns like Southampton." Eventually, in 1583, he set sail to take possession of his imaginary colonial empire, but after exploring Newfoundland he was forced by a variety of mishaps to return to England. During the course of a violent storm on the voyage home, his ship, the *Squirrel*, foundered, and Sir Humfrey and his crew were drowned. With him, needless to say, perished the whole grandiose fantasy. Yet again, America had turned out to be a delusion.

Perhaps the greatest disappointments of all, however, accompanied the first British attempts to settle in Virginia. The year after Sir Humfrey's death, his half-brother, Sir Walter Raleigh, dispatched a reconnaissance mission to the coast of North Carolina under the command of Captains Philip Amadas and Arthur Barlow. Their account of what they found is one of the classics of Renaissance travel literature. In a letter, passages of which found their way into Raleigh's poem "The Ocean's Love to Cynthia" and Michael Drayton's ode "To the Virginian Voyage," they assured their enthusiastic patron that Virginia was a land "of incredible abundance." The soil was "the most plentiful, sweet, fruitful and wholesome of all the world"; and as to the native Americans, "a more kind and loving people" could not be found on the face of the earth. But once again the vision faded as soon as the explorers tried to grasp it. When an expedition under the command of Sir Richard Grenville attempted to establish a settlement in Virginia in 1585, it soon discovered that Roanoke Island was no garden of Eden. On the contrary, food was hard to grow in any quantity, and the local inhabitants showed every sign of being suspicious if not actively hostile. After running short of the former and alienating the latter, the colonists sailed back to England with Sir Francis Drake in July of 1586, leaving behind them a handful of men who were never heard from again. The expedition of 1587, which culminated in the famous lost colony, was no less disastrous, and even when a permanent colony was finally established in Jamestown in 1607, the Utopian vision still stubbornly refused to come true. The land which Drayton had referred to in his ode as "earth's only paradise" was in reality a harsh and savage wilderness. Far from producing harvests "without your toil," as he had imagined, it demanded intense and skillful cultivation. In the New World as in the Old, man could eat bread only, as the Book of Genesis had it, in the sweat of his face.

That Monstrous World

Reinforced by the vivid descriptions of the American wilderness in Puritan writings of the early colonial period, this negative image of the New World persisted well into the eighteenth century, when it became one of the central issues in the great debate triggered by the publication in 1749 of the Comte de Buffon's *Natural History*. One of the most influential scientists of his day, Buffon believed that in America "animated Nature is weaker, less active, and more circumscribed in the variety of her productions" than in Europe. Basing his argument on the supposed paucity of both the human and the animal population of the New World, he theorized that on the other side of the Atlantic there must be "some combination of elements and other physical causes . . . that opposes the amplification of animated Nature." The combination of elements he finally settled upon was the coexistence in the American climate of a high level of moisture with a low level of heat. "In these melancholy regions," Buffon continued, "everything languishes, corrupts, and proves abortive. The air and the earth, overloaded with humid and noxious vapors, are unable either to purify themselves, or to profit by the influences of the sun, who darts in vain his most enlivening rays upon this frigid mass, which is not in a condition to make suitable returns to his ardor. Its powers are limited to the production of moist plants, reptiles, and insects, and can afford nourishment only to cold men and feeble animals."

Buffon's thesis was taken up and developed by a number of subsequent commentators, among them the Dutch-born scholar Cornelius de Pauw, author of the *Philosophical Investigations of the Americans* (1768-69), and the great Scottish historian William Robertson, who declared in his *History of America* (1777) that the early settlers could hardly have failed to find their adopted country anything but "waste, solitary, and uninviting." To the eighteenth-century European sensibility the newness of the New World clearly denoted not so much innocence and purity as immaturity and savagery. "When the English began to settle in America," Robertson observed grimly, "they termed the countries of which they took possession the wilderness. Nothing but their eager expectation of finding mines of gold could have induced the Spaniards to penetrate through the woods and marshes of America, where, at every step, they observed the extreme difference between the uncultivated face of nature and that which it acquires under the forming hand of industry and art."

Not that this view of the New World as a primitive, uncultivated wasteland inimical to all human civilization was allowed to go unchallenged for very long. In 1770 Frederick the Great's librarian, Dom Pernety, published his *Dissertation on America and the Americans* in which he claimed that if only de Pauw had been able to visit the country he had criticized so severely in his *Philosophical Investigations* he would surely have changed his mind. And after the events of 1776 a veritable flood of European writers hailed the United States as the "hope of the human race," in Jacques Turgot's famous phrase. In France the Marquis de Condorcet and the Marquis de Chastellux, in Germany Christoph

Ebeling and Friedrich von Gentz, in England William Blake and Percy Shelley all agreed that, in the latter's words:

> There is a people mighty in its youth,
> A land beyond the oceans of the west,
> Where, though with rudest rites, freedom and truth
> Are worshipped. . . .
> Yes, in the desert there is built a home
> For freedom. Genius is made strong to rear
> The monuments of man beneath the dome
> Of a new heaven. (*The Revolt of Islam*, 1818)

But despite the best efforts of its defenders and advocates, America continued to be portrayed in European poetry and prose in terms reminiscent of Buffon's *Natural History*. Just a year after Shelley had published the lines I have just quoted, for example, another English Romantic poet, John Keats, included the following description of the American landscape in his *Lines to Fanny*:

> Where shall I learn to get my peace again?
> To banish thoughts of that most hateful land,
> Dungeoner of my friends, that wicked strand
> Where they were wreck'd and live a wrecked life;
> That monstrous region, whose dull rivers pour,
> Ever from their sordid urns unto the shore,
> Unown'd of any weedy-haired gods;
> Whose winds, all zephyrless, hold scourging rods,
> Iced in the great lakes, to afflict mankind;
> Whose rank-grown forests, frosted, black, and blind,
> Would fright a Dryad; whose harsh herbag'd meads
> Make lean and lank the starv'd ox while he feeds;
> There bad flowers have no scent, birds no sweet song,
> And great unerring Nature once seems wrong.

In Keats' imagination America seems to have been a dreadful kind of anti-paradise, an infernal prison which had more in common with the nightmarish scenery of Dante's underworld than with Ovid's vision of the Golden Age. The ideal garden, flowing with milk and honey, was transformed into a barren wilderness doomed to eternal decay and sterility.

The American Eden

By the time Charles Dickens came to write his *American Notes* (1842) and the American chapters of his novel *Martin Chuzzlewit* (1844), based on his recent travels around the United States, a new and still more sinister element had entered the picture. For America was represented in these works neither as a paradise nor as a wilderness, but as a wilderness masquerading as a paradise. In Dickens' eyes this country was evidently a vast confidence trick perpetrated on the innocent inhabitants of Europe, a deliberate conspiracy to defraud the rest of the world by pretending to be the perfect society that the first explorers believed they had found. In both the journal and the novel this accusation is supported by a veritable plethora of evidence, but one instance in particular clearly stood out in Dickens' mind above all the rest: the case of an infamous settlement on the Mississippi called Cairo. It had been advertised in Europe as a prosperous city, full of opportunities for profitable investment and professional advancement, but when Dickens visited it by steamboat he found, in his own words, "a breeding-place of fever, ague, and death; vaunted in England as a mine of Golden Hope, and speculated in, on the faith of monstrous representations, to many people's ruin. A dismal swamp, on which the half-built houses rot away: cleared here and there for the space of a few yards; and teeming, then, with rank unwholesome vegetation, in whose baleful shade the wretched wanderers who are tempted hither, droop, and die, and lay their bones . . . a hotbed of disease, an ugly sepulchre, a grave uncheered by any gleam of promise: a place without one single quality, in earth, or air, or water, to commend it: such is this dismal Cairo."

Here, as many scholars have remarked, is the source of that marvelously ironic episode in *Martin Chuzzlewit* in which Martin and Mark are persuaded to invest all their savings in an exciting new development called Eden, only to discover upon their arrival that the one thing it has in common with the biblical home of Adam and Eve is that it is infested with snakes. The American version of Eden is nothing more than a fetid swamp inhabited by a few wretched immigrants who stay there only because they are either too poor or too weak to return. Once again the terrestrial paradise has turned out to be a cruel illusion. On this occasion, however, the illusion has not simply been projected across the Atlantic by the wish-fulfillment fantasies of Europe. It has been deliberately fostered and exploited by America herself. Europe may have cooperated in its own deception, but the plain fact is that it has been cheated.

Worse still, even when the fraud has been exposed, its authors refuse to admit that it is a fraud. When Mark has the temerity to remark in the presence of Mr. Chollop that the supposedly thriving city of Eden is just a hideous swamp, he is informed that "the sentiment is quite Europian [sic]," and when Dickens himself pointed out to his American

The Thriving City of Eden as it appeared on Paper by Hablôt Knight Browne. (Illustration in original edition of Charles Dickens' *Martin Chuzzlewit*.)

companions that such gross deceits as Cairo could hardly fail to bring their country into disrepute, he was given to understand that "this was a very smart scheme by which a deal of money had been made: and that its smartest feature was that they forgot these things abroad, in a very short time, and speculated again, as freely as ever." In Dickens' America, as Martin Chuzzlewit discovers for himself over and over again, "smartness" is a synonym for fraud, and a "bold speculator" is likely to be a man possessed of "a most distinguished genius for swindling." So although virtually everyone he meets during his travels is introduced to Martin as "one of the most remarkable men in our country, sir," gifted with a "moral sense" of almost superhuman sensitivity, virtually everyone ultimately reveals himself to be a liar, a cheat, or a scoundrel. What emerges from this novel, in short, is a picture of a society in which everyone is on the make but no one will admit it, a society in which the constantly reiterated professions of morality are simply a smoke screen for the most unscrupulous forms of public and private doubledealing. The country which has set itself up as the champion of liberty, Dickens never tires of pointing out, is also the home of slavery; the nation which proclaims so loudly the virtue of equality treats many of its own inhabitants as if they were subhuman.

In a society so deeply permeated by dissimulation and hypocrisy, the one thing that cannot be tolerated, needless to say, is the plain truth. Hence, as the one decent American whom Martin encounters, Mr. Bevan, points out to him shortly after his arrival, "No satirist could breathe this air. If another Juvenal or Swift could rise up among us tomorrow, he would be hunted down. . . . In some cases I could name to you, where a native writer has ventured on the most harmless and good-humored illustrations of our vices or defects, it has been found necessary to announce, that in a second edition the passage has been expunged, or altered, or explained away, or patched into praise." Presumably, the chief function of such a refusal to admit criticism is to avoid exposing the confidence trick in which Dickens believes America to consist. But there is more than a hint in the novel that a still more corrupting force is at work in America's reluctance to face the truth about itself, namely the urge to succumb to its own propaganda. Thus in his final judgment on the country he has just left, Mark Tapley declares on board the boat back to England that if he were a painter, he would never have chosen the eagle as the national symbol of the United States. " 'No,' said Mark, 'that wouldn't do for me, sir. I should want to draw it like a Bat, for its short-sightedness; like a Bantam, for its bragging; like a Magpie, for its honesty; like a Peacock, for its vanity; like an Ostrich, for its putting its head in the mud and thinking nobody sees it.' "

The Thriving City of Eden as it appeared in Fact by Hablôt Knight Browne. (Illustration in original edition of Charles Dickens' *Martin Chuzzlewit*.)

Illusion and Reality

The observations of another eminent literary Englishman of the nineteenth century, Matthew Arnold, pick up this theme and develop it still further. For the chief burden of his bad-tempered and supercilious essay *Civilization in the United States* (1888) is not merely that there is none, but that America persistently refuses to acknowledge the fact, even to itself. According to Arnold, the great American vice is not deception; it is self-deception. "The want [of beauty and interest in the United States]," he asserts,

> is graver because it is so little recognized by the mass of Americans; nay, so loudly denied by them. . . . But now the Americans seem, in certain matters, to have agreed, as a people, to deceive themselves that they have what they have not, to cover the defects in their civilization by boasting, to fancy that they well and truly solve, not only the political and social problem, but the human problem too. . . . The thrill of awe, which Goethe pronounces to be the best thing humanity has, they would fain create by proclaiming themselves at the top of their voices to be "the greatest nation upon earth," by assuring one another, in the language of their national historian, that "American democracy proceeds in its ascent as uniformly and majestically as the laws of being, and is as certain as the decrees of eternity."

In words reminiscent of Machiavelli's warning against idealistic speculations, Arnold concludes: "They see things not as they are, but as they would like to see them be; they deceive themselves totally. And by such self-deception they shut against themselves the door to improvement. . . . In what concerns the solving of the social and the political problem they see clear and think straight; in what concerns the higher civilization they live in a fool's paradise."

The twentieth-century equivalent of this view is the popular European image of the United States as a make-believe culture whose spiritual centers are Madison Avenue and Hollywood, and whose high priests are admen and moviemakers. If we are to believe many recent commentators, the fabrication of popular illusions has become the major industry of contemporary America. Political candidates, to take the most prominent example, are frequently portrayed as mere actors, obediently reciting the lines that have been written for them by their speech writers and expounding the policies which their managers have determined will have the broadest appeal to the electorate. Religious observances too, it is often objected, have been reduced by American evangelists to vulgar exercises in showmanship; as the British protagonist of Evelyn Waugh's *The Loved One* learns to his amusement, liturgy in this country "is the concern of the stage rather than of the clergy." Even the educational process has been suspected of harboring an unhealthy concern for appearances. To a cynical European visitor it might well appear that the grading system (eliminating *D*s and *F*s) initiated a few years ago at several American universities is a mechanism specifically designed to conceal any evidence of intellectual inadequacy on the part of their students. Defined as "a record of achievement," the academic transcript in such institutions has no place for non-achievement. Failure quite literally does not exist; like Augustine's definition of evil, it is a privation, an absence which has no objective reality. For in many cases, the lowest grade that can be recorded indicates "satisfactory work," and anything less than satisfactory is consigned to academic oblivion. American students are able to do well, better, or best, but they can not do badly—or if they do, no one apart from themselves and their professors can know about it. So far as the public record is concerned, everyone succeeds.

This to be sure is an extreme case, but a foreign observer might plausibly argue that it is symptomatic of a more widespread assault upon the traditional distinction between illusion and reality. Television advertisements regularly assure us that artificial orange juice tastes better than the natural stuff, that sausages and bacon made from textured vegetable protein are healthier than anything which came from a pig, and that synthetic egg-substitute is superior to the heart-stopping ovoids produced by hens. The doctor's office where we learn the folly of ignoring these appeals is likely to be furnished with glowing "wood" panels which are actually made of plastic, thick "woolen" carpet woven from synthetic fiber, rich "leather" chairs covered in vinyl, and in the corner a luxuriant machine-made "plant." As we drive back home past the false fronts and multinational facades of our local townscape, we may be forgiven for feeling that the difference between appearance and reality, original and imitation, is on the verge of breaking down completely. In the United States of the 1970s, authenticity is rapidly becoming as rare and as precious as oil.

This Great Stage

This general sense of unreality is reinforced to a considerable extent by another much-commented-upon feature of American civilization: the fact that buildings in this country do not seem to have been designed to last very long. The predominant impression which most of them convey is one of impermanence, and as Geoffrey Gorer has remarked, the impression is usually accurate. Returning to the United States in 1963 after an absence of only thirteen years, he found that "the centers of many cities in the United States have been far more radically reconstructed than have the most completely war-devastated towns in Europe that I know."

To an American sensibility this constant renewal of the urban and suburban environment appears to be not only natural but thoroughly desirable, for it is a visible sign of progress. In one of the most revealing scenes of Nathaniel Hawthorne's novel *The Marble Faun* (1860), for instance, the American narrator is appalled by the notion that so many of the buildings he sees in Rome have endured for so many centuries. A thousand years, he comments,

> would seem but a middle age for [many of] these structures. They are built of such huge, square stones, that their appearance of ponderous durability distresses the beholder with the idea that they can never fall, never crumble away.... But gazing at them, we recognize how undesirable it is to build the tabernacle of our brief lifetime out of permanent materials, and with a view to their being occupied by future generations. All towns should be made capable of purification by fire or of decay, within each half century. Otherwise they become the hereditary haunts of vermin and noisomeness, besides standing apart from the possibility of such improvements as are constantly introduced into the rest of man's contrivances and accommodations.

"You should go with me to my native country," one of the American characters remarks to an Italian shortly afterwards. "In that fortunate land each generation has only its own sins and sorrows to bear. Here, it seems as if all the weary and dreary Past were piled upon the back of the Present." For both Hawthorne and his characters, the physical perpetuation of the past in Europe clearly represents a degree of social and cultural stagnation that amounts to a kind of living death.

In the eyes of the Europeanized Henry James, on the contrary, the temporariness of American buildings is equally destructive to the human spirit. When he returned to this country in 1904 after a self-imposed exile of almost a quarter of a century, he fancied that he could hear the houses of New York telling him: "We are only instalments, symbols, stop-gaps ... expensive as we are, we have nothing to do with continuity, responsibility, transmission, and don't in the least care what becomes of us after we have served our present purpose." The major theme of his great travelogue *The American Scene* (1907) is that he had come back to a disposable culture, dedicated to change for its own sake and symbolized by the "impudently new" skyscrapers of Manhattan: "Crowned not only with no history, but with no credible possibility of time for history," he wrote, "and consecrated by no uses save the commercial at any cost, they are simply the most piercing notes in that concert of the expensively provisional into which your supreme sense of New York resolves itself. They never begin to speak to you, in the manner of the builded majesties of the world as we have heretofore known such—towers or temples or fortresses or palaces—with the authority of things of permanence or even of things of long duration. One story is good only till another is told, and sky-scrapers are the last word of economic ingenuity only till another word be written." After the monumental longevities of Europe, he was horrified by the transitoriness of the physical and moral landscape of his native land. America seemed to him to be caught up in what he called "a perpetual repudiation of the past," a self-conscious refusal to create anything that was not temporary. "You are perpetually provisional," he declared. "The hotels and the Pullmans . . . represent the states and forms of your evolution and are not a bit, in themselves, more final than you are." He was surrounded, he felt, by a society in which everything was still in process, and nothing appeared to be stable, finished, enduring.

As a result, to return to my earlier point, nothing appeared to him to be quite real. For in Europe one of the crucial tests of reality has always been duration. Illusions are evanescent, almost by definition, whereas truth, according to the ancient legend, is the daughter of time. A building which has survived for several centuries thus seems to be more indubitably *there* than one which has existed only for a paltry decade or two. Looked at from this point of view the American scene does rather resemble a stage set which may be struck and replaced with an entirely new one at any moment—hence the sense of unreality that Dickens expressed so memorably in his *American Notes*. "All the buildings," he wrote of Worcester, Massachusetts, "looked as if they had been built and painted that morning, and could be taken down on Monday morning with very little trouble. . . . The clean cardboard colonnades had no more perspective than a Chinese bridge on a teacup, and appeared equally well calculated for use." Even the White House in Washington, he claimed, had "that uncomfortable air of having been made yesterday." But it was when Dickens first stepped onto American soil at Boston that the illusionary quality of the scene struck him most forcibly. "The air was so clear," he noted, "the houses were so bright and gay; the sign boards were painted in such gaudy colors;

the gilded letters were so very golden, the bricks were so very red, the stone was so very white, the blinds and area railings were so very green, the knobs and plates upon the street doors so marvelously bright and twinkling; and all so slight and unsubstantial in appearance—that every thoroughfare in the city looked exactly like the scene in a pantomime."

Nor is this view of the United States confined to European or Europeanized writers. In *The Day of the Locust* (1939), written less than a decade before Evelyn Waugh's *The Loved One*, the American novelist Nathanael West depicts a world in which the barrier between the apparent and the real has broken down completely. Los Angeles, as he describes it, is a huge film set, its inhabitants a crowd of extras whose clothes bear not the slightest resemblance to their occupations: "A great many of the people wore sports clothes which were not really sports clothes. Their sweaters, knickers, slacks, blue flannel jackets with brass buttons were fancy dress. The fat lady in the yachting cap was going shopping, not boating; the man in the Norfolk jacket and Tyrolean hat was returning, not from a mountain, but an insurance office; and the girl in slacks and sneakers with a bandanna around her head had just left a switchboard, not a tennis court." The houses are no more genuine than the people who occupy them. As he gazes at "the Mexican ranch houses, Samoan huts, Mediterranean villas, Egyptian and Japanese temples, Swiss chalets, Tudor cottages, and every possible combination of these styles that lines the slopes of the canyon," the hero, Tod (whose name in German means death), notices that "they were all of plaster, lath and paper." "Steel, stone and brick," he muses, "curb a builder's fancy a little, forcing him to distribute his stresses and weights and to keep his corners plumb, but plaster and paper know no law, not even that of gravity." The setting of this novel is clearly a monstrous sham, destined to collapse as surely as the lath and plaster hill up which Napoleon's army prematurely charges in one of West's great comic set pieces. The counterparts of Dickens' disillusioned immigrants are now the American masses themselves, the characters who, in the terrible riot which forms the story's climax, set the whole city on fire when they realize that they have been tricked by the impostures of the image makers. It was for them that West gave the book its original title, *The Cheated*.

The Kingdom of the Dead

A still more devastating literary embodiment of this vision of America is Evelyn Waugh's notorious novel *The Loved One* (1948), written shortly after the author had visited Hollywood to arrange for the filming of one of his earlier works. It has often been treated as if it were a

A Transfer by Peter Blake.

straightforward satire on the grotesqueries of the American funeral industry in general and Forest Lawn in particular. I would like to suggest, however, that *The Loved One* is rather more than a fictional precursor of Jessica Mitford's exposé *The American Way of Death*. For the novel's central symbol, Whispering Glades, finally comes to represent not just Forest Lawn but the entire culture surrounding that beautifully manicured cemetery. In classical legend, as Waugh certainly knew, the Elysian fields across the western ocean were the abode of the dead, and this association, towards which the narrator points us with his repeated references to Greek mythology, lies at the very heart of *The Loved One*. Its British protagonist, Dennis Barlow, may come from what he believes to be a "dying world," but the one in which he finds himself in the opening chapter is already defunct, a vast "necropolis" peopled by the living dead. There is not very much difference, after all, between the corpses that Mr. Joyboy, the chief mortician at Whispering Glades, so skillfully transforms into grinning travesties of their former selves and the unfortunate Hollywood actress Baby Aaronson who, we learn from Dennis' uncle, has been successfully remodeled by the studio technicians as a sultry Latin beauty called Juanita del Pablo and a roguish but still nameless Irish colleen. At one level her transformation may be seen as a hideous parody of the process whereby the immigrant discards his or her national identity—Mr. Medici likes to be called Mr. Medissy because pronounced the first way his name "kinda sounds like a wop." At another level it might suggest the zombie-like quality of most of the book's characters. "Did you see the photograph some time ago in one of the magazines of a dog's head severed from its body, which the Russians are keeping alive for some obscene Muscovite purpose by pumping blood into it from a bottle?" asks Sir Frank Hinsley at one point. "It dribbles at the tongue when it smells a cat. That's what all of us are, you know, out here. The studios keep us going with a pump. We are still just capable of a few crude reactions—nothing more. If we ever got disconnected from our bottle, we should simply crumble." But at the deepest level of all the biography of Baby Aaronson seems to me to be a parable about a society caught up in a perpetual repudiation of its true nature, a society in which what you seem to be is infinitely more important than what you are.

The basic dichotomy between appearance and reality is forced upon our attention at the very outset by means of one of Waugh's most elaborate and successful jokes at his readers' expense. This is how the story begins:

> All day the heat had been barely supportable but at evening
> a breeze arose in the West, blowing from the heart of the set-

ting sun and from the ocean, which lay unseen, unheard behind the scrubby foothills. It shook the rusty fringes of palm-
leaf and swelled the dry sounds of summer, the frog-voices, the
grating cicadas, and the ever present pulse of music from the
neighboring native huts.

In that kindly light the stained and blistering paint of the
bungalow and the plot of weeds between the veranda and the
dry water-hole lost their extreme shabbiness, and the two Englishmen, each in his rocking-chair, each with his whiskey and
soda and his outdated magazine, the counterparts of number-
less fellow-countrymen exiled in the barbarous regions of the
world, shared in the brief illusory rehabilitation.

Coming to this novel from the exotic African settings of many of
Waugh's other works, *Scoop* and *Black Magic* to name only the best
known, we are naturally tempted to believe that this story too is going
to be set in some far-flung outpost of the British Empire. The two
Englishmen, Sir Frank Hinsley and his nephew Dennis Barlow, look and
sound like a pair of nineteenth-century colonial administrators desperately trying to maintain a semblance of Anglo-Saxon civilization in the
midst of a tropical jungle inhabited by primitive tribesmen. In fact, of
course, the native huts are the decayed mansions of a run-down Los
Angeles suburb, the pulsing music is not the beat of the tom-toms but
the swing of a popular dance band, and Sir Frank Hinsley, far from
being a representative of Her Britannic Majesty's Government, is chief
scriptwriter for Megalapolitan Pictures Inc. of Hollywood.

Like most of Waugh's jokes, however, this one has an ironic back-
lash to it. For as we read on we gradually realize that our first response
was the correct one after all, that the suburbs of Los Angeles *are* a
jungle and that the people who live and work in them *are* savages.
Beneath the bland civilities of the social surface Waugh reveals a sub-
stratum of violence and cruelty quite as savage as anything he has portrayed in his African novels. The only difference is that this is a jungle
that is trying to pass itself off as a civilization. Outwardly all is gentility,
courtesy, comfort, and hygiene—the world of Wilbur Kenworthy, the
founder of Whispering Glades, and Guru Brahmin, the pseudonymous
author of an advice column in a local newspaper. Inwardly all is vul-
garity, cruelty, corruption—the world of Mr. Schultz, who runs an
animal cemetery modeled on Whispering Glades, and Mr. Slump, a
cynical newspaperman. What makes it so disturbing, in Waugh's eyes,
is that in the one case metaphorically and in the other case literally they
are the same man. The high-minded dreamer who saw "a vision of all

that art and nature could offer to elevate the Soul of Man" in Whispering Glades is the same Wilbur Kenworthy who at an annual dinner for his employees defined his creation as "a dog's toilet and a cat's motel." And the Guru Brahmin who utters the saccharine pieties of his correspondence column is the Mr. Slump who callously dismisses the novel's heroine as "a prize bitch" and drunkenly advises her to "go take a high jump," which she obligingly does.

The firing of Sir Frank Hinsley, with its extraordinary combination of evasiveness and ruthlessness, is a marvelous example of the fundamental hypocrisy that produces such schizoid characters. For not until he forces the issue is anyone at Megalapolitan Studios so forthright as to tell him that his services are no longer required. Instead, he is subjected to an increasingly painful series of rebuffs which eventually bring him to the realization that, in the traditional euphemism, his contract is not being renewed. First he is advised to take a week's holiday; then he is told that neither a secretary nor a chauffeur is available when he needs one; and finally he finds his old office occupied by a total stranger. The irony of all this, of course, is that the whole humiliating process is an essentially benevolent subterfuge, designed to avoid confronting Sir Frank directly with the fact of his dismissal—and so to sustain the illusion that this is a society in which nobody loses his job.

The same motive is evident in the way in which virtually all the characters in *The Loved One* address each other. In the opening chapter Sir Frank Hinsley tells his nephew that "people out here . . . talk entirely for their own pleasure," but that is not quite true. They talk for each other's pleasure too. Language, in this novel, has degenerated into mere euphemism, a form of verbal cosmetic whose chief function is to conceal the often ugly realities to which it is applied. Words, as most of Waugh's characters use them, are instruments of misrepresentation rather than communication, ways of evading such disturbing facts as sex, pain, death, and human intolerance: "I presume your Loved One was a Caucasian," remarks an attendant at Whispering Glades. "No, why did you think that?" Dennis replies. "He was purely English." "English are purely Caucasian, Mr. Barlow," she corrects him. "This is a restricted park. The Dreamer has made that rule for the sake of the Waiting Ones. In their time of trial they prefer to be with their own people." "I think I understand," remarks Dennis. "Well, let me assure you, Sir Francis was quite white." A veil of clinically antiseptic jargon seems to have descended over the entire human landscape. Occasionally, though, the veil slips, and we are given a disconcerting glimpse of the cynicism that lies beneath it. Shortly after the interchange I have just quoted, for instance, the same attendant utters the following testimonial to the skill of Mr. Joyboy and his assistants: "We had a Loved One last month who was found drowned. He had been in the sea a month and they only identified him by his wristwatch. They fixed that stiff . . . so he looked like it was his wedding day. The boys up there surely know their job. Why if he'd sat on an atom bomb they'd make him presentable." For a moment it is as if Mr. Slump had unexpectedly emerged from behind the figure of Guru Brahmin. But only for a moment. Immediately afterwards, Waugh notes, the attendant slips on her professional manner again "as though it were a pair of glasses."

And in a sense that is precisely what it is, a pair of rose-tinted spectacles. For the point that Waugh is making through such episodes, hilarious though they are, is a profoundly serious one. The idealistic expectations which Europe has projected upon America from the moment of its discovery onwards have created in this country, he implies, a deep-seated urge to maintain that it really is as ideal as it is expected to be. Rather than disappoint itself or Europe it chooses to deceive them, to keep up an appearance of Edenic excellence by ignoring or glossing over any unpleasant facts that might call the myth into question. By doing so, Waugh insists, American culture has committed itself to denying the two most basic facts of human nature, sex and death. According to the biblical story of the Fall of Man, Adam and Eve's disobedience in the garden of Eden had two immediate results. They became aware for the first time of their sexuality and they became subject to mortality. In the artificial paradise Waugh describes in *The Loved One*, both of these consequences are treated as if they were nonexistent. Even though Aimée Thanatogenos, the book's nominal heroine, brushes her hair with a perfume called "Jungle Venom" ("From the depths of the fever-ridden swamp," the advertisement for it reads, "where juju drums throb for the human sacrifice, Jeanette's latest exclusive creation, Jungle Venom, comes to you with the remorseless stealth of a hunting cannibal"), she is absolutely outraged if any of her suitors dares to behave in appropriately primitive fashion. She condemns both Dennis' behavior and the sensual outpourings of the English love poets as "unethical," and complains to Guru Brahmin that they sometimes make her "feel unethical too." In order to be even remotely acceptable, Dennis learns, the erotic impulse has to be as carefully packaged as any commercial product. "The English poets," Waugh comments wryly, "were proving uncertain guides in the labyrinth of Californian courtship. . . . Dennis required salesmanship."

If sexuality is concealed in the world of this novel, mortality is positively obliterated. People in *The Loved One* do not die; they pass on, and a great deal of care is taken to evade the physical fact of death. During the elaborately staged charade of the funeral parlor, the last sight the bereaved are given of the corpse is "as they knew [it] in buoyant life, transfigured with peace and happiness." At Whispering Glades no wreaths or other depressing memorials are permitted, and Sir Frank is allowed to meet his Maker accompanied by a floral tribute made up in the shape of crossed cricket bats and wickets only because, in Dr. Kenworthy's judgment, "the trophy was essentially a reminder of life, not of death." So when Dennis quotes to Aimée the great line from Keats' *Ode to a Nightingale*, "To cease upon the midnight with no pain," she is deeply moved for perhaps the only time in the novel. "That's exactly what Whispering Glades is for, isn't it?" she whispers. As Geoffrey Gorer puts it in *The American People*, "The elaborate art of the morticians, the cosy beauty of the funeral parlors, and the landscaping of the gardens of rest have attempted to remove from death most of its poignancy, and most of its meaning." In the kingdom of the dead, reminders of death are inadmissible.

According to Gorer, the American attitude towards death is just one example of "the system of achieving morality by treating as nonexistent facts which cannot be reconciled" with the ethical structure you wish to believe in—which takes us, of course, back to my original point of departure, Christopher Columbus on Hispaniola. For Dickens, Arnold, Gorer, and Waugh are all in their different ways suggesting, I think, that in his refusal to admit that the land he had discovered was anything other than the land he had wanted to discover, Christopher Columbus was indulging in what was destined to become the great American pastime: he was living in a fool's paradise.

Spring Turning by Grant Wood.

CHAPTER THREE

THE OPEN SOCIETY

Before I built a wall I'd ask to know
What I was walling in or walling out,
And to whom I was like to give offense.
Something there is that doesn't love a wall,
That wants it down.

Robert Frost, "Mending Wall," in *North of Boston*, 1914

ONE OF THE MOST IMPORTANT duties Dennis Barlow is called upon to perform in *The Loved One* is to make the arrangements for the burial of his uncle, Sir Frank Hinsley, in Whispering Glades. The funeral service has been assigned to the University Church there, and while Dennis is inspecting it to make sure that everything is ready for the ceremony, he takes the occasion to listen to a recorded lecture provided by the cemetery's proprietors for the benefit of tourists. This is what he hears:

> You are standing in the Church of St. Peter-without-the-walls, Oxford, one of England's oldest and most venerable places of worship. Here generations of students have come from all over the world to dream the dreams of youth. Here scientists and statesmen still unknown dreamed of their future triumphs. Here Shelley planned his great career in poetry. From here young men set out hopefully on the paths of success and hap-

piness. It is a symbol of the soul of the Loved One who starts from here on the greatest success story of all time. The success that waits for all of us whatever the disappointments of our earthly lives.

This is more than a replica, it is a reconstruction. A building again of what those old craftsmen sought to do with their rude implements of by-gone ages. Time has worked its mischief on the beautiful original. Here you see it as the first builders dreamed of it long ago.

You will observe that the side aisles are constructed solely of glass and grade A steel. There is a beautiful anecdote connected with this beautiful feature. In 1935 Dr. Kenworthy was in Europe seeking in that treasure house of Art something worthy of Whispering Glades. His tour led him to Oxford and the famous Norman church of St. Peter. He found it dark. He found it full of conventional and depressing memorials. "Why," asked Dr. Kenworthy, "do you call it St. Peter-without-the-walls?" And they told him it was because in the old days the city wall had stood between it and the business center. "*My* church," said Dr. Kenworthy, "shall have no walls." And so you see it today full of God's sunshine and fresh air, birdsong and flowers. . . .

Waugh's image of a wall-less church incorporates two of the most persistent themes I have encountered in European commentary on the American value system. The present chapter will be concerned with the first of them, the following chapter with the second.

People in Glass Houses

When the American novelist and essayist Mary McCarthy visited the Italian city of Florence, among the first things she noticed were the walls. "Many Florentine palaces today," she wrote in her delightful travel book *The Stones of Florence* (1959), "are quite comfortable inside and possess pleasant gardens, but outside they bristle like fortresses or dungeons, and, to the passing tourist, their thick walls and bossy surfaces seem to repel the very notion of hospitality." Her observation tells us as much about her own sensibility, I believe, as it does about the phenomenon she is describing, for although what she says is certainly true of Florence (as it is of many other European cities), a visitor from England, France, Germany, or Spain would scarcely have considered it worthy of comment. A European would simply have taken it for granted that the palaces of Florence, like any other civilized human habitation, should be constructed in such a way that their exteriors

A Bigger Splash by David Hockney.

protected their occupants from the prying eyes of passing tourists. Only an American visitor, I suspect, would have found it at all remarkable that the palaces of Florence should appear uninviting when viewed from the outside.

The reason, needless to say, is that buildings in the United States do not, as a rule, repel the gaze of the passerby. On the contrary, they often seem specifically designed to attract it, and as a result one finds European writers constantly pointing out with evident astonishment that American houses are not usually walled off from the outside world. The inhabitants of the newly discovered lands across the Atlantic, wrote Peter Martyr in 1511, live in "a golden age; neither ditches nor hedges, nor walls enclose their domains; they live in gardens open to all." He was describing, of course, a nonurban society, but his observation has been repeated by many commentators on the modern American urban scene. The Irish wit James Hannay, for instance, contrasts what he calls the Englishman's "almost morbid love of privacy" with the American's willingness to be viewed by others. Whereas "the first thing an Englishman does when he builds a house is to surround it with a high wall," he notes in *From Dublin to Chicago* (1914), "the Americans do not build walls around their houses. The humblest pedestrian going afoot through the suburbs of Philadelphia, Indianapolis, or any other city, sees not only the houses but anything in the way of a view which lies beyond them." And Geoffrey Gorer, writing some thirty years later, remarks: "In the normal American house . . . nearly everything is open to the inspection of the world; no hedges, walls, or gates separate the building from the road."

According to most European observers, moreover, the same is true of the interiors of American houses. As the protagonist of Kingsley Amis' novel *One Fat Englishman* (1963) passes from the living room to the kitchen, the British narrator thus pauses to explain that "the place was one of those ranch-type affairs that of course left doors off to promote togetherness." Hannay claims that "walls outside houses are like doors inside. The European likes both because the desire for privacy is in his blood. The American likes neither." And Gorer remarks upon "the absence of doors in all but the most private parts of most houses, the wedged-open doors of offices and studies." To judge from these comments, the patron saint of American architects might well have been Joshua.

The Importance of Being Earnest

Various explanations have been offered to account for this lack of exclusory or separative structures. Amis, as we have just seen, assumes that its purpose is "to promote togetherness" while Hannay attributes it to "the wonderful sociability of the [American] people." At one point in his analysis Gorer takes a similar view, though he defines it negatively as a "fear of loneliness" as opposed to a positive disposition towards sociability. But later, when he encounters the identical feature in public buildings, Gorer provides a quite different explanation: "The glass-walled office skyscrapers soar into the clear air, transparent by day, an illuminated fairyland by night. . . . It seems as if such transparency has also a symbolic significance. It is a demonstration to all the world that nothing wrong, nothing subversive is going on inside this glass case, everything is quite literally open and above board; . . . [These buildings] are shining symbols of the soaring, aspiring, transparent integrity which Americans like to think—and not without justification—is their most praiseworthy characteristic."

This last interpretation seems to me to take us rather more deeply into the question than do the diagnoses of Amis and Hannay. For what Gorer is getting at here is what many commentators regard as *the* American value: openness, whether personal or institutional. To begin with the first, virtually every description I have read of the American character includes the word "open," "frank," "sincere," or "earnest." Here, for instance, is a representative selection drawn chiefly from Henry S. Commager's invaluable anthology *America in Perspective* (1947): "Kind, frank and sensible, . . . always free to communicate what they know" (William Cobbett, 1818); "frank, brave, cordial, hospitable" (Charles Dickens, 1842); "frank, communicative, sincere" (Alexander Mackay, 1846); "clear . . . frank . . . earnest" (Salvador de Madariaga, 1928); "sincere . . . friendly" (John Buchan, 1940); "open, friendly" (Simone de Beauvoir, 1947). The belief that everything is, or should be, apprehensible to the outside world thus seems to have led to the establishment of sincerity as the dominant norm governing personal relationships in this country, at least as Europeans perceive it. Sincerity, after all, is simply a form of human transparency. A sincere person is an individual-without-the-walls, a self that allows you to see into its interior. In the presence of such a person, one feels assured, nothing is being concealed, nothing is being held in reserve or masked by a veil of irony, understatement, or wit—the three favorite modes of European discourse.

One obvious manifestation of this reverence for candor is the cult of informality in American dress and American speech—the almost immediate use of first names, for instance, rather than the more distant, impersonal modes of address. For first names, like casual clothes, suggest ease, openness, the frankness of familiarity, whereas formality im-

New York Interpreted, III: The Skyscrapers by Joseph Stella.

plies reserve and consequently a certain degree of concealment. Another less obvious manifestation of the same impulse may be a phenomenon that puzzled me for a long time after my arrival in this country, namely the fact that puns, which are so prized in Great Britain, are generally greeted by Americans with groans of disapproval. The reason, I have come to suspect, is that any form of *double entendre* reminds us that words as well as people are capable of having hidden meanings, that the very language we use to communicate with each other is not always completely "sincere."

Be that as it may, a European visitor to the United States very quickly learns that nothing is regarded with greater suspicion by the great majority of Americans than any hint of affectation. In *The Catcher in the Rye*, the most damning word in Holden Caulfield's vocabulary was "phony," and after the charges we have seen such writers as Dickens, Arnold, and Waugh leveling at America it is not hard to understand why. A nation that has been accused so consistently of playacting could hardly fail to be especially sensitive on this point. Anything smacking of overt dissimulation is bound to seem particularly threatening to an illusionistic society that insists on pretending to be real. So when Roger Micheldene, the British hero (if that is the word) of Amis' *One Fat Englishman*, offers a beautifully polished critique of the commercialization of religion in the United States, his American antagonist, Irving Macher, reproves him not for the opinions he has just expressed but rather for the quasi-dramatic mode of their delivery. "Pretty competent, sir," he observes, "but overly scripted, wouldn't you say? A little lacking in spontaneity. . . . Some of the ideas you were propounding just now came pretty close to the way I feel. My objection was you gave the whole thing too much production. Sounded rehearsed. And that means it probably was rehearsed. . . . It's just that I like people to behave naturally, without looking to the effect all the time. To me, that's behaving like a human being, living by impulse. . . . And what you say sounds to me like a performance."

The attitudes subsumed in Macher's speech are evident in many of the distinctive speech mannerisms of American English, especially in the almost compulsive use of the word "really" in everyday conversation and the obsessive recourse to the phrase "you know" as a stopgap in any sentence that involves a pause, or even in one that doesn't—"I really, you know, would like to see a movie, you know, but they're all really terrible this week, you know." It is as if the speaker were trying to force comprehension upon the person he or she is addressing, as if both the authenticity of the feeling being revealed and the speaker's success in communicating it had to be incessantly reasserted to guarantee their continuance. There must be no walls between people, these habits seem to be suggesting, and if there must be walls let them at least be of glass.

At the political and institutional level, the openness of this country has long been proverbial in Europe. For Jean-François Revel, it is reflected most clearly in the extraordinary degree of freedom that the public media enjoy in the United States. "When something happens in America," he writes in his provocative tract *Without Marx or Jesus*, "the media cover every detail of the event: a Mafia scandal in New Jersey, with political implications; illegal betting on football games; the financial wheeling and dealing of a former secretary to the Senate Majority. There is never any 'Mr. X.' Names are given, and photographs, and details about the crime, and the amounts of money involved. On the series of programs about the F.B.I. [broadcast in January 1970], for instance, former agents of that agency appeared in person to explain and criticize certain operations in which the rights of citizens had clearly been violated." This last example is particularly revealing in light of the disclosures that have been made still more recently. In no other nation in the world, I think it is fair to say, would the clandestine activities of its internal and external security agencies have aroused such profound and widespread abhorrence as they have in the United States. If there was ever any doubt about the matter, the American people's response to the secretiveness of their own secret services has amply demonstrated that concealment of any kind is an affront to a deeply held national principle.

Yet paradoxically, this very insistence on plain dealing in every area of public and private life may well have been responsible for the power that those agencies acquired in the first place. For in a society so firmly committed to the belief that the table is the place for one's cards, the figure who provokes the fiercest antipathy is likely to be the subversive, the individual with secret political loyalties hidden up his sleeve. Subversives, to be sure, are disliked and feared in other countries too, but in America they seem to touch an especially raw nerve in the body politic. Indeed, one of the reasons that McCarthyism flourished so vigorously here, I have always suspected, was that it tapped this phobic reaction to all forms of concealment. In the 1950s at least, many Americans were evidently willing to put up with what in Europe would have been regarded as intolerable invasions of their privacy simply to ensure that no pockets of subversiveness, real or imaginary, remained unexposed. As Richard Nixon discovered to his cost, in a nation that places **such a high value on sincerity the one unforgivable crime is deceit.**

The Magic of Numbers

According to some of the most perceptive European commentators, the set of attitudes I have just been describing may well explain why American society has so often been accused of being materialistic. It is not, they insist, that Americans are any more acquisitive or possessive than the inhabitants of Europe. It is simply that in the United States the exceptional importance given to openness has created a profound suspicion of any kind of value that is not outwardly visible. To the American sensibility, that is to say, there appears to be something potentially sinister about the notion of intrinsic worth, of unquantifiable quality, in a word, of class. As the British journalist George W. Steevens noted in *The Land of the Dollar* (1898), "Americans are the most demonstrative of all the peoples of the earth. Everything must be brought to the surface, embodied in a visible, palpable form. . . . It is in this sense that the Americans may fairly be called the most materialistic people of the world. Materialistic in the sense of being avaricious, I do not think they are. . . . But materialistic, in the sense that they must have all their ideas put in material form, they unquestionably are."

George Santayana amplifies on Steevens' point in his *Character and Opinion in the United States*. "The most striking expression of this materialism," he writes,

> is supposed to be [the American's] love of the almighty dollar; but that is a foreign and unintelligent view. The American talks about money because that is the symbol and measure he has at hand for success, intelligence, and power; but as to money itself, he makes, loses, spends, and gives it away with a very light heart. To my mind the most striking expression of his materialism is his singular preoccupation with quantity. If, for instance, you visit the Niagara Falls, you may expect to hear how many cubic feet or metric tons of water are precipitated per second over the cataract. . . . Nor is this insistence on quantity confined to men of business. The President of Harvard College, seeing me once by chance soon after the beginning of a term, inquired how my classes were getting on; and when I replied that I thought they were getting on well, that my [students] seemed to be keen and intelligent, he stopped me as if I was about to waste his time. "I meant," said he, "what is the number of students in your classes."

"Here," comments Santayana, "I think we may perceive that this love of quantity often has a silent partner, which is diffidence as to quality.

The democratic conscience recoils before anything that savors of privilege; and lest it should concede an unmerited privilege to any pursuit or person, it reduces all things as far as possible to the common denominator of quantity. Numbers cannot lie."

Bigness, after all, is a convenient metaphor for goodness. Quantity is more easily measurable than quality, and for the numerical sensibility that Santayana describes, the temptation to equate wealth with virtue and poverty with wickedness may be hard to resist. In *Martin Chuzzlewit*, for instance, the hero learns to his surprise that there is an aristocracy in America, and when he inquires of what it is composed, he is told, "Of intelligence, sir, of intelligence and virtue. And of their necessary consequence in this republic. Dollars, sir." Given this assumption, it is only to be expected that, as Martin discovers shortly afterwards during the course of an after-dinner conversation with a group of American businessmen, "all their cares, hopes, joys, affections, virtues, and associations seemed to be melted down into dollars. . . . Men were weighed by their dollars, measures gauged by their dollars; life was auctioneered, appraised, put up, and knocked down for its dollars."

A less notorious but equally striking consequence of the exteriority of American values is the quite remarkable importance attached in this country to physical hygiene. Over and over again the novelists and essayists I have been quoting include a scene such as the following one from Waugh's *The Loved One:* "With a steady hand Aimée fulfilled the prescribed rites of an American girl preparing to meet her lover— dabbed herself under the arms with a preparation designed to seal the sweatglands, gargled another to sweeten the breath, and brushed into her hair some odorous drops from a bottle labelled: 'Jungle Venom.'" In the words of a current soap advertisement, "It isn't enough to *be* clean; you've got to *smell* clean." Hygiene, like justice, must be seen (or scented) to have been done. External freshness is a sign of internal purity—occasionally, the commentators hint, a substitute for it.

Privacy and Personality

As some of these comments reveal, Europeans are frequently somewhat uneasy when they first encounter the emphasis on exteriority in American culture. The reaction of the French journalist Raoul de Roussy de Sales to the openness with which married couples are accustomed to deal with each other in the United States is an excellent case in point. When an American marriage shows any signs of strain, he asserts in his delightful essay *Love in America* (1938), "various attempts at readjustment are made with devastating candor. Married couples seem to spend many precious hours of the day and night discussing what is wrong with their relationship. The general idea is that—according to the teachings of most modern psychologists and pedagogues—one should face the truth fearlessly. Husbands and wives should be absolutely frank with one another, on the assumption that if love between them is real it will be made stronger and more real still if submitted, at frequent intervals, to the test of complete sincerity on both sides."

"This is a fine theory," he continues, "but it has seldom been practiced without disastrous results. There are several reasons why this should be so. First of all, truth is an explosive, and it should be handled with care, especially in married life. It is not necessary to lie, but there is little profit in juggling with hand grenades just to show how brave one is. Secondly, the theory of absolute sincerity presupposes that, if love cannot withstand continuous blasting, then it is not worth saving anyway. Some people want their love life to be a permanent battle of Verdun. When the system of defense is destroyed beyond repair, then the cause of hopeless maladjustment is invoked by one side, or by both. The next thing to do is to divorce and find someone else to be recklessly frank with for a season."

Returning to his native country thirty years earlier, Henry James, too, was appalled by its "large mistrust of privacy." America had become, he argued in *The American Scene*, "the land of the open door." To the "restored absentee," as James called himself,

> the universal custom of the house with almost no one of its indoor parts distinguishable from any other is an affliction against which he has to learn betimes to brace himself. This diffused vagueness of separation between apartments, between hall and room, between one room and another, between the one you are in and the one you are not in, between the place of passage and the place of privacy, is a provocation to despair which the public institution shares impartially with the luxurious "home." . . . Thus we have the law fulfilled that every part of every house shall be, as nearly as may be, visible, visitable, penetrable, not only from every other part, but from as many parts of as many other houses as possible, if they only be near enough. Thus we see systematized the indefinite extension of all spaces and the definite merging of all functions; the enlargement of every opening, the exaggeration of every passage, the substitution of gaping arches and far perspectives and resounding voids for enclosing walls.

After reading this passage one can hardly help wondering what James would have said had he lived to see the apotheosis of the open-plan house, the California Eichler.

The reason James deplored this trend in American architecture so vehemently was that in his view, walls, whether physical or psychological, were essential if any sense of human individuality was to survive in the twentieth century. As he put it, the houses he was describing "testify at every turn, then, to [the disposition] of the American people, to the prevailing 'conception of life'; they correspond, within doors, to the as inveterate suppression of almost every outward exclusory arrangement. The instinct is throughout, as we catch it at play, that of minimizing, for any 'interior,' the guilt or odium or responsibility, whatever these may appear, of its *being* an interior. The custom rages like a conspiracy for nipping the interior in the bud, for denying its right to exist, for ignoring and defeating it in every possible way, for wiping out successively each sign by which it may be known from an exterior." For James, the private, interior world of the self with its secrets, its mysteries, its hidden complications and ambivalences was inviolate. As a result he was profoundly shocked and threatened by the tendency he identifies in these passages to do away with the distinction between the interior and the exterior, to break down the psychological walls between the self and the world. "Letting it all hang out" he would have regarded, quite literally, as a form of self-annihilation, and it is no accident that one of his most powerful short stories, *The Aspern Papers*, concerns the attempt by an American scholar to obtain from the aging mistress of a great poet the letters that her lover had written to her during the course of their affair. For in his relentless, unscrupulous campaign to pry into the intimate details of someone else's life, the nameless American researcher who tells the story is acting out James' lifelong nightmare of the assault on the *sanctum sanctorum* of the private self.

Much the same attitude can be detected in Dickens' criticism of the American press in *Martin Chuzzlewit*. The basis of his complaints is not, as we might have expected, that newspapers in this country do not provide very full or very accurate news but rather that they provide the wrong kind of news, namely the personal affairs of individual citizens. "Here's the *Sewer's* exposure of the Wall Street Gang, and the *Sewer's* exposure of the Washington Gang," cries a New York newsboy in the novel, "and the *Sewer's* account of a flagrant act of dishonesty committed by the Secretary of State when he was eight years old; now communicated at great expense, by his own nurse." Shortly afterwards, when Martin is shown a copy of another paper by its proprietor, Colonel

Diver, and is asked for his opinion of it, he replies, "Why, it's horribly personal." The colonel, Dickens comments, "seemed much flattered by this remark; and said he hoped it was." In the eyes of many European writers, the freedom and energy of the American press which so impressed Revel clearly have another and less attractive side.

A Self-with-the-Walls

By far the most radical challenge I have encountered to this value system, however, is Vladimir Nabokov's notorious novel *Lolita* (1955). In a brief but important afterword the expatriate Russian novelist claims that he is trying very hard "to be an American writer." Just what he means by this is not immediately clear, for on the previous page he has vigorously disavowed the two kinds of fiction which, rightly or wrongly, most Europeans associated with this country in the 1950s, namely the hairy-chested Hemingwayesque novel written, as Nabokov puts it, "in short, strong, realistic sentences (He acts crazy. We all act crazy I guess. I guess God acts crazy etc.)" and the stern, moralistic novel of the post-Hawthorne school; "*Lolita*," we are assured, "has no moral in tow." I would suggest that what Nabokov means when he asserts that he is trying to be an American writer is simply that *Lolita* belongs to a subspecies of the novel that appeals more directly than any other to the taste for openness I have been analyzing: the confessional novel.

Subtitled *The Confession of a White Widowed Male*, the story is related in the first person by Humbert Humbert, a middle-aged neurotic of Anglo-Swiss descent who has immigrated to America in order to qualify for a substantial inheritance. Once here he seduces a young "nymphet," the Lolita of the title, gains access to her by marrying her mother, Charlotte Haze, but later loses her to a still more sinister character, Clare Quilty, whom Humbert Humbert eventually murders in a futile attempt to regain his lost Lolita. The book is ostensibly being written while Humbert is waiting to go on trial. Addressing his readers as "ladies and gentlemen of the jury," he apparently wishes to make a clean breast of his crimes in the hope that to understand all will lead us to forgive all.

Thanks to the largely unflattering portrait it paints of the United States, *Lolita* was reviled by many of its early reviewers for being rabidly anti-American, a charge that Nabokov himself strenuously denied. But unless I am very much mistaken the novel *is* anti-American, though at a much more fundamental level than the reviewers imagined. For it seems to me that Humbert Humbert and his creator are playing an elaborate joke on an audience accustomed to forthright self-revelation. In the prologue, attributed to a fictional professor of English, John Ray Jr., we are told that there is "a desperate honesty that throbs through [Humbert's] confession," but in fact the entire story is an elaborate exercise in self-concealment designed to tantalize and ultimately frustrate what Nabokov takes to be the distinctively American passion for candor. Humbert Humbert, that is to say, is only pretending to confess, only simulating the openness he assumes his audience demands. Far from making himself transparent, he is doing everything in his power to preserve his opacity.

A number of passages in the novel point toward this conclusion. At one point, for instance, Lolita's mother bares her innermost feelings for Humbert Humbert. "I know how reserved you are, how British," she writes during the course of a long and embarrassingly candid letter to him. "Your old-world reticence, your sense of decorum, may be shocked by the boldness of an American girl. You who conceal your strongest feelings must think me a shameless little idiot for throwing open my poor bruised heart like this." Shortly afterwards, however, when Humbert Humbert has finally married her, she makes the mistake of demanding the same degree of outspokenness from him. In a scene reminiscent of de Sales' account of marital encounter sessions, Humbert Humbert tells us that "She showed a fierce insatiable curiosity for my past. She desired me to resuscitate all my loves so that she might make me insult them, and trample upon them, and revoke them apostately and totally, thus destroying my past. She made me tell her about my marriage to Valeria, who was of course a scream; but I also had to invent, or to pad atrociously, a long series of mistresses for Charlotte's morbid delectation. To keep her happy, I had to present her with an illustrated catalogue of them, all nicely differentiated . . . the languorous blond, the fiery brunette, the sensual copperhead—as if on parade in a bordello. The more popular and platitudinous I made them, the more Mrs. Humbert was pleased with the show."

From a character such as this we would surely be wise to take any alleged confessions with more than a grain of salt, to recognize at least the possibility that he is doing to us what he did to Charlotte and what, in an earlier scene, we saw him doing to his American psychiatrist. "I owe my complete restoration [from a mental breakdown]," Humbert informs us, "to a discovery I made while being treated at that particular very expensive sanatorium. I discovered there was an endless source of robust enjoyment in trifling with psychiatrists: cunningly leading them on; never letting them see that you know all the tricks of the trade; inventing for them elaborate dreams, pure classics in style (which make them, the dream-extortionists, dream and wake up shrieking); teasing them with fake 'primal scenes'; and never allowing them the slightest glimpse of one's real sexual predicament." Here if anywhere, I would suggest, is the key to Nabokov's overall strategy in this novel. First he lures us into treating *Lolita* as if it really were, in the words of John Ray Jr.'s introduction, "a case history," and then he proceeds to tease us too with enigmatic "libidreams," fake "primal scenes," and a host of readily identifiable (but in the context of the story totally baffling) Freudian symbols. Not until we reach the afterword does he reveal his "old feud with Freudian voodooism," a feud in which, by our readiness to play the role of analyst, we have cast ourselves temporarily as his antagonists.

There are also plenty of false clues for the would-be literary critic, for literary interpretation is the other major form of analysis that Nabokov is seeking to subvert in this book. The play in which Lolita performs, for instance, is entitled "The Hunted Enchanters" while the name of the motel in which Humbert Humbert first seduces her is "The Enchanted Hunters," and the address left by Clare Quilty in another motel register is an anagram of the same words: Ted Hunter, Cane, NH. But none of the clues add up to a solution, all the patterns turn out to be meaningless, and we are left at the end of the story as completely in the dark as we were at the beginning. "Everybody should know," Nabokov declares in his afterword, "that I detest symbols and allegories . . . [and the] generalizations devised by literary mythists and sociologists." "Teachers of literature," he chides us, "are apt to think up such problems as 'what is the author's purpose?' or still worse 'what is the guy trying to say?' " As critics no less than as psychiatrists we have been led all too willingly up Nabokov's garden path.

The reason that Nabokov singles out these two activities for special obloquy, I believe, is that both literary and psychological analysis are based upon what many Europeans have identified as the fundamental fallacy of American culture: the notion that human beings and their artifacts are ultimately comprehensible. As a practitioner of the first kind of analysis, I must admit that Nabokov may have a point as far as our attitude to literature is concerned. For no word is dearer to American literary critics than the word "key" (I used it myself a short while back), as if our metier were to unlock poems rather than to enjoy them. Whereas critics in England generally tend to concentrate on the appreciation and evaluation of the works they treat, we in this country often act like intellectual safecrackers, determined to reveal to the rest of the world whatever secrets may lie behind a writer's verbal combinations. Our basic inclination, in other words, is to regard literary works of art as puzzles whose solutions would be attainable if only we could learn to read the clues properly, or, to change the metaphor slightly, as cryptograms which we could break if only the right code books were available.

According to at least one commentator, the same impulse was at work in the enthusiastic reception that Freud's psychological theories were given in the United States. "One of the greatest moral revolutions that ever happened to America," writes Raoul de Roussy de Sales in the essay I quoted earlier, "was the popularization of Freud's works. . . . Here at last was a system that explained fully why love remained so imperfect. It reduced the whole dilemma of happiness to sexual maladjustments, which in turn were only the result of the mistakes made by one's father, mother, or nurse, at an age when one could certainly not be expected to foresee the consequences. Psychoanalysis integrated human emotions into a set of mechanistic formulas. One learned with great relief that the failure to find happiness was not irreparable. . . . Love could be made to work like anything else." Freud's theories thus held out the prospect of actually understanding people, of explaining their irrationalities and phobias, of breaking down the walls of repression and anxiety that they had erected around themselves and seeing them for what they really were.

Nabokov, on the contrary, insists on our essential mysteriousness, on the impenetrability of human consciousness. By creating a protagonist who actually resists comprehension while pretending to invite it, he has mounted a frontal assault upon the belief that men and women are explicable. The only revelation his novel has to make is the revelation Hamlet makes to Rosencrantz and Guildenstern, the Renaissance forerunners of all those modern sociologists, psychologists, opinion pollsters, and questionnaire framers who would seek to penetrate our hidden center: "Why look you now, how unworthy a thing you make of me! You would play upon me; you would seem to know my stops; you would pluck out the heart of my mystery; you would sound me from my lowest note to the top of my compass; and there is much music, excellent voice, in this little organ, yet cannot you make it speak. S'blood, do you think I am easier to be played on than a pipe? Call me what instrument you will, though you can fret me, you cannot play upon me."

Here, I would suggest, speaks the ageless voice of European humanism, the voice we can hear being echoed in the repeated protests by European writers against the tendency they perceive in this country to tear aside every veil, to probe every secret, unravel every enigma— against what Santayana calls "the habit of regarding existence as a riddle, with a surprising solution which we think we have found."

"Nature," he declares in the same chapter, "is like a beautiful woman that may be as delightfully and as truly known at a certain distance as upon closer view; as to knowing her through and through, that is nonsense in both cases, and might not reward our pains." There is more to this comment than mere male chauvinism, though there is certainly a good deal of that. Beneath it one can catch, I think, the distinctive European acceptance of, and reverence for, the unknown, the mysterious, the obscure. One can catch it, too, in this description of Dennis Barlow's reaction to American women in *The Loved One*: "She was convenient; but Dennis came of an earlier civilization with sharper needs. He sought the intangible, the veiled face in the fog, the silhouette at the lighted doorway, the secret graces of a body which hid itself under formal velvet. He did not covet the spoils of this rich continent, the sprawling limbs of the swimming pool, the wide-open painted eyes and mouths under the arc lamps."

As these passages reveal, the European sensibility is profoundly uneasy in an Eden in which no knowledge is forbidden, where nothing is allowed to remain concealed, unspoken, unrevealed. For a world in which everything is openly displayed can finally come to seem rather two-dimensional to a mind that is accustomed to acknowledging the existence and value of unfathomed and unfathomable depths in the human personality. To be transparent, after all, is to run the risk of being completely invisible: when someone has seen through us, we are, in a sense, no longer there, for our identity depends upon our retaining at least a certain degree of opacity. So although the determination to leave no depths unplumbed, no stone unturned, no possibility unexplored, has no doubt created in America the most advanced and exciting technological society in the history of the world, it is also arguable that it has robbed us of at least a part of our humanity, the private sanctuary of a self-with-the-walls.

Landscape near Fort Laramie by Frank Buchser.

CHAPTER FOUR

SWEET LAND OF LIBERTY

Nothing is more favorable to nourishing successful seeds of liberty in Americans than the land they inhabit. Spread far and wide in an immense continent, free as the nature that surrounds them, among the crags and the mountains, the vast plains and the deserts, at the edge of forests where all is still wild, where nothing reminds them of servitude or man's tyranny, they encounter the lessons of liberty and independence in all the physical objects about them.

Joseph Mandrillon, *The American Spectator*, 1784, translated by H.S. Commager and Elmo Giordanetti

IN THE PRECEDING CHAPTER I talked as if walls were purely exclusory structures, as if their sole function were to keep things *out*. In fact, of course, they also serve to keep things *in*, to enclose as well as to exclude, to restrict as well as to protect. They stand, in other words, not only for security but also for confinement. As a result, the relative absence of walls in the domestic, social, and moral architecture of the United States has a second and equally complex series of ramifications for the European sensibility encountering it.

Forbidden Waters

Perhaps the best way of getting at these ramifications is to remind ourselves at the outset of a simple but absolutely crucial historical fact, namely that the very discovery of America consisted in the successful defiance of a limit which had previously been regarded as impassable. As we all learned at school, the pillars of Hercules, the modern straits of Gibraltar, were thought in the Middle Ages to mark the point beyond which mankind was forbidden to venture to the West. So when Dante inquires why Ulysses is languishing in the eighth circle of Hell in *The Divine Comedy*, he learns that the legendary Greek hero has come to grief because he refused to accept those divinely imposed limits on his experience. Not even his love for his family, Ulysses explains:

> Could conquer the inward hunger that I had
> To master earth's experience, and to attain
> Knowledge of man's mind, both the good and the bad. . . .
> I and my crew were old and stiff of thew
> When at the narrow pass we could discern
> The marks that Hercules set far in view
> That none should dare beyond, or further learn. . . .
> "Brothers," I said, "who manfully, despite
> Ten thousand perils have attained the West,
> In the brief vigil that remains of light
> To feel in, stoop not to renounce the quest
> Of what may in the sun's path be assayed,
> The world that never mankind hath possessed.
> Think on the seed ye spring from! Ye were made
> Not to live life of brute beasts of the field
> But follow virtue and knowledge unafraid."

Only two centuries later, sentiments such as these were to become almost commonplace, but to a medieval reader they must have seemed little short of blasphemous. For the hero of the *Odyssey* was proposing not merely to sail into forbidden waters but to transgress the limits that God in his wisdom had imposed on human understanding. Ulysses was reaching out once again, as it were, for the fruit of the tree of knowledge.

It was in this general context that the poets of the sixteenth century saw the discovery of America. According to another Italian poet, Torquato Tasso, the voyage of Columbus was considerably more than a perilous venture into the unknown; it was another attempt to break through the physical and intellectual boundaries originally challenged by Ulysses. "Great Hercules," wrote Tasso in his epic *Jerusalem Delivered* (1575), "durst not assay the ocean main":

> Within his pillars would he have impal'd
> The over-daring wit of mankind vain;

Till Lord Ulysses did those bounders pass,
To see and know he so desirous was;

He passed those pillars, and in open wave
Of the broad sea first his bold sails untwined,
But yet the greedy ocean was his grave,
Naught helped him his skill gainst tide and wind;

"The time shall come," Tasso then announces, wise after the event, "that sailors shall disdain":

To talk or argue of Alcides strait;
And lands and seas that nameless yet remain,
Shall well be known, their bounders, site and seat. . . .

A knight of Genes [Genoa] shall have the hardiment
Upon this wondrous voyage first to wend [go],
Nor winds nor waves that ships in sunder rent,
Nor seas unused, strange clime, or pool unkenned [unknown],
Nor other peril nor astonishment
That makes frail hearts of men to bow and bend
Within Abila's strait shall keep and hold
The noble spirit of this sailor bold.

What in the fourteenth century had been an example of "the over-daring wit of mankind vain" is now an expression of "the noble spirit" of a "sailor bold." Ulysses' hunger "to master earth's experience" is no longer a prideful challenge to God's authority, a reenactment of the original sin of disobedience in the garden of Eden. On the contrary, the quest for "the world that never mankind hath possessed" is a heroic act of liberation that has freed the human race from the confines of medieval superstition and ignorance. "I marvel," wrote Sir Martin Frobisher's biographer George Best, "that man, who hath always abhorred so much thraldom and restraint, and so greedily desired liberty, could be contented so many thousand years to be shut up in so narrow confines." For the men and women of sixteenth-century Europe, the primary significance of the discovery of America was that it demonstrated the possibility, perhaps even the desirability, of going beyond previously accepted perimeters. From the very beginning, violation of limit was perceived as the quintessential American act.

Unlimited Possibilities

As Edmundo O'Gorman has emphasized, the consequent expansion of Europe's horizons was intellectual as well as physical. Before they could even begin to comprehend just what it was that Columbus had really discovered, the geographers of the Renaissance had first to free themselves from a set of assumptions which had governed man's view of his world for at least the preceding millennium. For according to the late classical and medieval *Weltanschauung*, the three continents, Europe, Africa, and Asia, together comprised a kind of enormous island, the island earth or *orbis terrarum* as it was known, which was surrounded by ocean. The possibility of a fourth continent in the Northern Hemisphere was never seriously considered; the most that the Atlantic Ocean might contain, it was thought, was an undiscovered island or two. Indeed, the Christian doctrine of the descent of the entire human race from Adam and Eve appeared to rule out automatically the possibility of another large inhabited land mass on the terraqueous globe, since its existence would have posed the insoluble problem of explaining how the descendants of the first pair could have reached it. Only very gradually, then, did America come to be recognized for what it was. Not until the inhabitants of Europe had abandoned many of their most revered beliefs about the nature of the world they lived in could they reluctantly formulate the concept of a new world, an *orbis alter*.

O'Gorman sums up the results of this mental readjustment as follows:

> The moment that the *orbis terrarum* was conceived as transcending its ancient insular bounds, the archaic notion of the world as a limited space in the universe assigned to man by God, wherein he might gratefully dwell, lost its *raison d'être*. Since then man has been in a position to comprehend that his world really has no bounds because it is in any and every part of the universe of which he can possess himself. . . . The world having thus ceased to be considered as a sort of cosmic jail, man was able to picture himself as a free agent in the deep and radical sense of possessing unlimited possibilities in his own being, and as living in a world made by him in his own image and to his own measure. Such is the profound meaning of the historical process which we have called the invention of America. . . . It was not by coincidence that America came upon the historical stage as the home of liberty and of the future. American man was the new Adam of Western culture.

The discovery of America thus involved nothing less than an intellectual revolution in European thinking, the creation of an entirely new conceptual framework within which to accommodate the phenomenon of a new world. The metaphysical horizon had expanded quite as dramatically as the geographical one.

Wide Open Spaces

Something of the same sort seems to take place, albeit on a much smaller scale, in the experience of every individual immigrant or visitor who discovers America for himself. As early as the sixteenth century, notes R.L. Bruckberger, the explorers' exploits burst upon the consciousness of Europe like "a shell breaching prison walls. At last the imprisoned could escape; at last a corner of the world had been found where they could breathe easily and live as they pleased." Here, by way of comparison, is a passage from Michel de Crèvecoeur's *Letters from an American Farmer* (1782) describing what it felt like to arrive in this country for the first time over two hundred years later: "A European, when he first arrives," he wrote, "seems limited in his intentions, as well as in his views; but he very suddenly alters his scale; two hundred miles formerly appeared a very great distance, it is now but a trifle; he no sooner breathes our air than he forms schemes, and embarks on designs he never would have thought of in his own country. There the plenitude of society confines many useful ideas, and often extinguishes the most laudable schemes which here ripen into maturity. Thus Europeans become Americans."

This profound sense of release, of liberation, often begins, as in de Crèvecoeur's case, as a purely physical experience. One's whole sense of scale is suddenly transformed by the sheer dimensions of the New World. In the words of the German aesthetician Richard Müller-Freienfels, "The first characteristic of the external image of America [is] its different dimensions." "Spatially considered," he continues in his ambitious study *The Mysteries of the Soul* (1927), "the distance from New York to San Francisco is much greater than the distance from London to Leningrad, but psychically speaking the distance is trifling. No frontiers lie between them; the same language is spoken from the Atlantic to the Pacific; and there is no need to visit a money-changer. It is truly a continent that the traveler is crossing but it is also a country, and *one* country of stupendous dimensions. Its provincial cities are larger than many European capitals; its lakes are small seas, wider in area than a European kingdom; its agricultural land is not divided up into small parcels, but the cornfields cover the plains like a shoreless ocean. Everything has other dimensions than with us." Unpartitioned by either cultural or natural barriers, America seems boundless, limitless, inexhaustible, and the European visitor feels like a Lilliputian suddenly set down in the land of the Brobdingnags.

But one's sense of scale very quickly adjusts, as another German writer, Francis Lieber, has suggested it did in the case of the earliest settlers. Attempting to explain why "distances are not considered in this country as [they are] in Europe," he argues in his *Letters to a Gentleman in Germany* (1827) that "the early settlers had to think of many thousand miles off whenever they thought of their beloved homes. Thus a far different unit by which to estimate other distances was laid down in their minds. It is clear that a person settling a hundred miles from them could not appear far away to those who had their original home some thousand miles off." And this feeling, Lieber goes on to assert, created "a daring spirit of enterprise which gradually has settled down into a fixed trait of the American character." The frontier spirit, which Frederick Jackson Turner believed to be the source of the American people's restlessness and energy, may thus be a product of a still more deep-seated element in the national consciousness, the immigrant experience.

Whatever the merits of his concluding hypothesis, Lieber is surely right to emphasize the psychological consequences of the physical expansion that takes place in the immigrant's horizons when he first arrives in America. For the absence of spatial limitation in this country very soon translates itself into the absence of other modes of obstruction. One's mental vision, that is to say, expands together with one's physical vision, and projects which seemed quite out of the question in the Old World now seem perfectly feasible here in the New. One has, in short, an exhilarating sense of possibility, as if Ulysses' brief vision of human aspiration uncircumscribed by any boundary were about to come true. In a society-without-the-walls the vistas appear to be endless.

The Perpetual Revolution

European descriptions of this phenomenon invariably concentrate upon the two greatest obstacles to human self-fulfillment in any society: the threat to our personal independence posed by external authority and the restrictions placed upon our individual development by internal incapacity. To begin with the first, virtually every commentator I have read has proposed that one of the most obvious explanations for the sense of freedom I have been describing is the profoundly anti-authoritarian bias of American culture. The United States, they never tire of pointing out, was created by a whole series of challenges to external authority, the most famous being the Pilgrim fathers' refusal to conform to the doctrines and practices of the established church and the American revolutionaries' refusal to conform to the dictates of the British government.

This attitude has since been reinforced, if we are to believe Geoffrey

Gorer, by the rejection of paternal authority which the son of every immigrant has been encouraged to undertake in order to establish his own Americanness. "The more successful the immigrant father was in turning his children into Americans, so that they had no other allegiances or values," writes Gorer in *The American People*, "the more his foreignness became a source of shame and opprobrium, the less important did he become as a model and guide and exemplar. . . . It was this break of continuity between the immigrants of the first generation and their children of the second generation which is to my mind of major importance in the development of the modern American character, which gave rise to what might be called, by analogy with genetics, the American mutation." Needless to say, sons have rebelled against their fathers in other cultures too, but in those cases, Gorer claims, "the rejection of the father as a guide and model was a private solution to a personal problem; in the United States it was also an act which symbolized the acceptance of the dominant values of the society to which they had pledged allegiance. The individual rejection of the European father as a model and a moral authority, which every second-generation American had to perform, was given significance and emphasis by its similarity to the rejection of England by which America became an independent nation." So when Jefferson declared his liking for "a little rebellion now and then" and Walt Whitman exhorted his fellow countrymen to "resist much, obey little," they were enunciating what Gorer takes to be a fundamental if unwritten principle of American society.

That some such principle is at work is suggested by the suspicion with which all authority figures are viewed in this country. Nothing seems to be regarded with greater hostility by the vast majority of Americans than the naked exercise of authority, whether it be by a policeman, a government official, a parent, or even a college professor. In the public realm in particular, Gorer remarks, "people in authority must be conspicuously plain citizens, with the interests and mannerisms of their fellows; whatever their private temperament, they must act like 'one of the boys,' glad-handed, extrovert, mindful of first names, seeing their subordinates in their shirt-sleeves, and with their feet on the desk, democratically obscene in their language, with private interests, if any, simple and within the reach of all."

Seen in this context, many of the characteristic idioms of American English take on fresh significance. Think, for instance, of all the linguistic strategies that have been developed in this country to avoid giving a direct command and thereby exercising overt authority. Where a British mother would say "Please pick up your toys," her American counterpart would be more likely to put it in one of the following ways: "Why don't you . . . " or "I'll let you . . . " or "Do you want to . . . " or simply, "How would you like to pick up your toys?" Grammatically, three of these expressions appear to be questions, but the mother would probably be somewhat taken aback if they were treated as such. For in reality they are imperatives disguised as interrogatives, ways of exerting authority without appearing to do so.

In both the public and the private realms, then, Americans seem to Europeans to be willing to take quite extraordinary precautions against giving even the *impression* of authoritarianism. Those who cannot, or will not, make the necessary effort immediately become the targets of determined attempts to demonstrate that they are not worthy of obedience anyway. It is this trait that Charles Dickens evidently had in mind when, in the concluding chapter of his *American Notes*, he asserted that American society was being undermined by "the universal distrust" of its citizens. "You carry," he wrote, "this jealousy and distrust into every transaction of public life."

> It has rendered you so fickle, and so given to change, that your inconstancy has passed into a proverb; for you no sooner set up an idol firmly than you are sure to pull it down and dash it into fragments; and this, because directly you reward a benefactor, or a public servant, you distrust him, merely because he *is* rewarded; and immediately apply yourselves to find out, either that you have been too bountiful in your acknowledgements, or he remiss in his deserts. Any man who attains a high place among you, from the President downwards, may date his downfall from that moment.

Dickens of course was describing this country as it existed in the middle of the nineteenth century, but to anyone who has witnessed the recent convulsions in the American body politic, his words can hardly fail to sound prophetic. The ongoing assault upon the hitherto inviolate memory of Camelot, in particular, suggests that in this respect at least the American national character has not changed very substantially over the past hundred years or so. If, as I suggested earlier, the fabrication of myths is a major American industry, their destruction seems to provide employment for an even larger work force.

According to Dickens, the basic iconoclasm of the United States was also reflected in its religious attitudes. "All Protestantism," Edmund Burke had noted at the time of the American Revolution, "even the most cold and passive, is a sort of dissent. But the religion most prevalent in our northern colonies is a refinement of the principles of resistance; it is the dissidence of dissent, and the Protestantism of the Protestant religion." Dickens agreed wholeheartedly, and like Burke he was careful to emphasize that this averseness "from all that looks like absolute government" was the effect, not the cause, of the American rejection of authority. "I cannot hold with other writers on these subjects," he announced, "that the prevalence of various forms of dissent in America is in any way attributable to the non-existence there of an established church: indeed, I think the temper of the people, if it admitted of such an Institution being founded amongst them, would lead them to desert it as a matter of course, merely because it *was* established."

This view of America as a nation of gainsayers in a state of perpetual revolution against its own political, religious, and social establishment is equally prevalent in Europe today. One has only to glance at the major European newspapers to find their political columnists commenting with evident bewilderment upon the American urge to prove that every idol has at least one foot of clay. Certainly the sheer amount of energy devoted to agonizing reappraisals of past events, searching reassessment of past policies, devastating reevaluations of past Presidents (not to mention the barrage of inquiries, investigations, and reviews in which the chief activity of the United States Congress seems to consist) has provided foreign observers with ample evidence in support of the popular European thesis that this is an essentially masochistic culture which enjoys nothing more than flagellating itself in public whenever it has the opportunity. Even as passionate an admirer of America as Jean-François Revel notes that it seems to be afflicted with "a widespread and strong feeling of guilt, and a passion for self-accusation which, on occasion, tends to go to extremes."

The major thesis of Revel's recent tract *Without Marx or Jesus*, however, is that in the 1960s, if not before, the "universal distrust" which Dickens detected in the American people has had overwhelmingly positive consequences. During the past decade, Revel claims, "the only new revolutionary stirrings in the world have had their origin in the United States. From America has come the sole revolutionary invention which can be described as truly original. I mean the complex of new oppositional phenomena designated by the term 'dissent.'" Protest, he goes on to argue, is of the essence of the American character, with the result that "America in 1971 is a mobile entity. It crosses all lines, not only financial, social, and familial lines, but also cultural and moral lines. . . . Crisis has become America's second nature. But in order to realize this fact, one must live it; and that is why the rest of the world perceives only dimly the true dynamism of present-day

America." Or as another French writer, Simone de Beauvoir, expresses in her travelogue *America Day by Day*, in America "I had the inspired feeling that anything might happen."

Liberty or License

The feeling de Beauvoir describes can obviously be extremely exhilarating, but for certain kinds of personality it can also be profoundly disturbing. For in the mind of a conservative European the continual challenge to authority in this country may conjure up the specter of complete lawlessness. Not surprisingly, in view of his comments on America's iconoclastic tendencies, Dickens' novel *Martin Chuzzlewit* provides a classic instance of this alternative response. The American definition of liberty, Dickens constantly implies, means not so much freedom from tyranny as freedom to tyrannize. Here, for instance, is his description of the aftermath of an American election which Martin witnesses just after landing in New York: "Some trifling excitement prevailed upon the very brink and margin of the land of liberty; for an alderman had been elected the day before; and Party Feeling naturally running rather high on such an exciting occasion, the friends of the disappointed candidate had found it necessary to assert the great principles of Purity of Election and Freedom of Opinion by breaking a few legs and arms, and furthermore pursuing one obnoxious gentleman through the streets with the design of slitting his nose." Nor, Dickens assures us, are such goings-on confined to the streets of New York. "Thus Martin learned . . . that to carry pistols into legislative assemblies, and swords in sticks, and other such peaceful toys; to seize opponents by the throat, as dogs or rats might do; to bluster, bully, and overbear by personal assailment were glowing deeds. Not thrusts and stabs at Freedom, striking far deeper into her House of Life than any sultan's scimitar could reach; but rare incense on her altars, having a grateful scent in patriotic nostrils, and curling upward to the seventh heaven of Fame. . . ."

In Dickens' nightmarish vision of America as a land where anything goes, liberty has been reduced to license, freedom has given way to anarchy, and the absence of circumscribing social and legal structures has permitted the growth of a lawless jungle in which every creature is free to prey on every other. This, to be sure, is an extreme as well as an outdated view, but contemporary European platitudes about the violence of American society suggest that Dickens' opinion is still widely held today.

A less dramatic, though equally common, version of the same basic complaint concerns the lack of material rather than moral or legal restraint in American culture. For viewed from an aesthetic standpoint, the American refusal to accept limits can readily be interpreted as an absence of good taste, which, according to the traditional European criterion, consists in proper proportion. To a sensibility informed by this standard, there seems to be in the United States a tendency to take things to extremes. Roger Micheldene's sentiments about a party to which he has been invited in Kingsley Amis' *One Fat Englishman* are fairly typical, I think, of the initial European reaction to the sheer exuberance of American style. Would the barge on which the party was to take place, he wonders, "turn out to be some funnelless yacht boasting a uniformed crew and two or three bars hung with abstract expressionist paintings? Rather more likely he would find middle-aged men in jeans and leather jackets doling out martinis from the middle of a waterlogged raft, an authentic Mississippi relic transported in sections across a thousand miles of land for the occasion. Could they never do things except by two-and-a-halves?"

In a more serious vein, Paul Bourget gave the following description of the houses he saw in Newport at the end of the nineteenth century:

> A first impression emerges from the homes of Newport. It ought to be correct, so much does it accord with the rest of American life, even outside of villas like these. This is a new evidence of excess, abuse, absence of moderation. On the floors of halls which are too high there are too many precious Persian and Oriental rugs. There are too many tapestries, too many paintings on the walls of the drawing rooms. The guest chambers have too many *bibelots*, too much rare furniture, and on the lunch or dinner table there are too many flowers, too many plants, too much crystal, too much silver.

The reason, he observes, is that "the American spirit seems not to understand moderation. Their high business buildings are too high. Their pleasure-houses are too elegant. Their fast trains go too fast. Their newspapers have too many pages; too much news. And when they set themselves to spend money, they are obliged to spend too much in order to have the feeling of spending enough."

Later in his essay, Bourget attributes such extravagance to the sheer energy of American civilization, whose tendency to excess he compares with that of the Italian Renaissance. Other commentators, more concerned with economic considerations, have pointed to the tremendous natural abundance that has always distinguished this country from most others. But I would suggest that American extravagance may also be an expression of the disposition I have been attempting to define in this chapter, the disposition which for Henry James was symbolized by a hotel in Palm Beach "proclaiming itself . . . with all the eloquence of an interminable towered and pinnacled and gabled and bannered skyline, the biggest thing of its sort in the world," and for Simone de Beauvoir by the skyscrapers of New York and Chicago. "The great attraction that America holds for me," she wrote in the final chapter of *America Day by Day*,

> consists in the fact that it appears as a realm still in transcendence; its history is contracted, of course, in time, yet stretches splendidly across vast spaces; it is the history of the creation of a whole world. For this reason skyscrapers always move me; they proclaim man as a being who does not stagnate, but is filled with enthusiasm and a desire for expansion and fresh conquest. In the shameless profusion of goods that you find in the drugstores there is poetry as fantastic as in a baroque church; man has taken matter in the raw in the toils of his desire, and declares the power of imagination over matter. New York, Chicago, both these cities reflect the existence of this demi-urge with its imperial dreams, and that is why they are indeed the most human, the most uplifting cities that I know. There is no room here for any of the dreary caution of the *petit bourgeois* in his carpet slippers, whose only object is to stay at home and wait for death, as the sonnet has it. To devote one's life to that is living death. Americans in this sense are truly alive; inertia does not appeal to them.

In the United States, one might say, nothing exceeds like excess.

The Perfectibility of Man

De Beauvoir's peroration touches on several of the issues involved in the second set of impediments to individual self-realization that I mentioned earlier, namely the restrictions imposed upon us by our personal inadequacies and incapacities. When Europeans write about American optimism, as they incessantly do, they usually mean that this form of limitation, too, is either denied altogether or at least severely challenged in the United States. Walls within us seem to be as inimical to the American system of values as walls around us.

Hence we find the tremendous emphasis on fulfillment in the passage from Evelyn Waugh's *The Loved One* that I quoted at the beginning of the previous chapter. I remarked at the time that his description of the church of St. Peter-without-the-walls summed up the two most

Still from *Metropolis* by Otto Hanke.

frequent observations to be made about this country by European writers. The transparency of the building was one of them. The perfectibility of man and his works is the other. The church itself, you may recall, was a "reconstruction," a "building again of what those old craftsmen sought to do with their rude implements of by-gone ages." Modern technology has enabled the workmen at Whispering Glades not merely to replicate the ancient Norman structure but to *perfect* it. "Here you see it," proclaims the guide, "as the first builders dreamed of it long ago." And what is true of the building is also true of the men and women whose funerals it accommodates. In the original St. Peter-without-the-walls, the students who came to worship there could only "dream the dreams of youth." In the improved trans-Atlantic version, the human soul embarks on "the greatest success story of all time. The success that waits for all of us whatever the disappointments of our earthly lives." As we listen to this speech with Dennis Barlow, we begin to realize that the words carved in the marble book at the entrance to Whispering Glades, "Enter stranger and be happy," sound more like a command than an invitation. Once inside, nothing less than absolute satisfaction, total success, will be expected of us. Wilbur Kenworthy's necropolis is clearly a place where dreams are bound to come true.

If, as I believe, Waugh intended Whispering Glades to be a symbol of the entire culture surrounding it, he has caught in these phrases one of the most distinctive elements in American culture as Europeans perceive it. In Italian, for instance, *fare l'America* means "to succeed" and according to Raoul de Roussy de Sales "success, the constant effort to make things work perfectly and the conviction that they can be made to, is the great national preoccupation. . . . In the American way of life there are no insoluble problems. You may not know the answer yourself, but nobody doubts that the answer exists—that there is some method or perhaps some trick by which all riddles can be solved and success achieved."

Just such a faith in the capacity of the human race to transcend its imperfections seems to me to be reflected in many of the characteristic speech idioms of this country, notably in the way in which the word "problem" is used. For whereas an Englishman might say "I am an alcoholic" or "I am chronically lazy," his American counterpart would be more likely to phrase it "I have a drinking problem" or "I have a problem with my study habits," thereby revealing two very reassuring assumptions: first, that the condition is somehow separable from the person afflicted by it, as if the problem were an undesirable virus which had by sheer ill chance settled upon one's character but for which one bore no real moral responsibility; second, that the condition is remediable, since the very notion of a problem suggests the existence of a solution, if only we could find it. By the same token, nobody in America is either poor or ignorant. They are only "economically disadvantaged" or "educationally handicapped," the passive participles suggesting once again that failure, intellectual as well as economic, is something that is done to you and therefore something that a more efficient and just social system can eventually correct.

At the root of these assumptions there lies, clearly enough, a profound and thoroughly un-European optimism. Indeed, I would like to propose that the dominant ethic in the United States is not the Protestant work ethic, upon which so much ink has so laboriously been spilled, but rather the pragmatic work ethic—by which I mean the belief that everything, including human beings and their relationships, can be made to work, to work, that is, in the sense of functioning properly. A small but typical example from my own experience may serve to illustrate the point. In Britain, on the rare occasions that my car ran smoothly, I used to feel that it was a brief and necessarily transitory victory won in the teeth of a world filled with unscrupulous manufacturers, dishonest salesmen, and incompetent mechanics. In this country, on the other hand, I learned to regard failure rather than success as the aberration; it was when my car did *not* run smoothly that something unusual seemed to be happening. And my expectations underwent a similar though more gradual reversal in the realm of human affairs. It was not inevitable, I slowly came to feel, that man and his products should always work imperfectly. If a well-adjusted automobile was not beyond the bounds of possibility, then neither was a well-adjusted person or a well-adjusted society. In short, I began to think like an American.

A New Beginning

Paradoxically, the cultural phenomenon that brought about my change of attitude may itself have been created by the cumulative experience of generations of immigrants who came to this country, as I did, in order to make a fresh start. American optimism, in other words, could very well be a product of the age-old European belief that the New World offers to everyone who is willing to take it the chance to make a new life. "What did [they] find in America that so captivated them?" asks R.L. Bruckberger of the earliest settlers. "Their delight lay in finding nothing," he replies. "They had to start afresh, on a continent they could not measure. . . . The settlers had to begin anew, as though they stood at the threshold of history." And for every immigrant who has come here ever since, America has continued to represent a personal, if not a social, clean slate, an opportunity to begin again.

To become an American, then, is to become a new man. As de Crève-coeur's classic definition reveals, the element of novelty is indispensable: "He is an American, who, leaving behind him all his ancient prejudices and manners, receives new ones from the new mode of life he has embraced, the new government he obeys, and the new rank he holds. . . . The American is a new man, who acts upon new principles; he must therefore entertain new ideas, and form new opinions." And by the same token, of course, he must also renounce his old ideas and opinions. "With very few exceptions," Gorer writes, "the immigrants did not cross the ocean as colonists to reproduce the civilization of their homes on distant shores; with the geographical separation they were prepared to give up, as far as lay in their power, all their past; their language and the thoughts which only that language could express, the laws and allegiances which they had been brought up to observe; the values and assured way of life of their ancestors and former compatriots; even, to a large extent, their customary ways of eating, of dressing, of living."

The process of acquiring an American identity may thus involve a transformation so profound that it can very easily take on quasi-religious overtones. "I was born, I have lived, and I have been made over," declares Mary Antin at the beginning of the autobiography she wrote shortly after immigrating to America. "Is it not time to write my life's story? I am just as much out of the way as if I were dead, for I am absolutely other than the person whose story I have to tell. . . . I could speak in the third person and not feel that I was masquerading. I can analyze my subject, I can reveal everything; for she, not I, is my real heroine. My life I have still to live; her life ended when mine began." The title of her book, *The Promised Land*, already suggests the basic metaphor through which she approaches her experience as an immigrant. Crossing the Atlantic has become the equivalent of crossing the Red Sea, the great symbolic act by which she has confirmed her liberation from Egyptian bondage and set her face toward the Holy Land.

In the works of several other writers, the transition from Europe to America sounds more like a return to the garden of Eden. As we saw in Chapter One, ever since America was first discovered it has been portrayed as a terrestrial paradise exempt from the ills of guilt-ridden, post-lapsarian Europe. The immediate corollary of this image of the New World is that the Old World immigrant is transfigured, upon his arrival, into a second Adam. By becoming an American he is able to regain his lost innocence, to cancel the effects of the Fall and live out the rest of his life free of the overwhelming burden of sinfulness and corruption which the Puritans summed up in the phrase "Original Sin" —hence General Choke's question in Dickens' *Martin Chuzzlewit*: "What are the great United States for, sir," he enquires, "if not for the regeneration of man?" Not surprisingly, no one has the temerity to answer him.

But although the immigrant experience makes rather good mythology, it makes very poor theology indeed. For implicit in the myth I have just been sketching are a number of assumptions which the church, Catholic as well as Protestant, has always considered to be thoroughly heretical. First, there is the belief that we can repudiate our individual and collective pasts, that the process which St. Paul defined as "putting off the old man" can take place as a result of merely human initiative. Orthodox Christian doctrine would insist, on the contrary, that we cannot simply leave our moral history behind us as if it were a country. The Atlantic is not a baptismal font, and its waters have no sacramental power. As far as our essential nature is concerned, we emerge from them unchanged.

Second, there is the concomitant belief that the immigrant's American offspring are born into a state of innocence comparable to that of Adam and Eve before the Fall. Uncontaminated by the effects of the forbidden fruit, the inhabitants of the New World are thus free to aspire to a level of moral, intellectual, and physical perfection which would be absolutely unthinkable anywhere east of the American Eden. So deeply ingrained has this faith in human perfectibility become that any suggestion that we may be limited by hereditary factors beyond our control is greeted by many Americans with immediate and intense hostility. The way in which Freud's psychoanalytical theories have been treated in this country is an excellent case in point, for their pessimistic initial premise, according to Gorer, "has been sloughed off, treated as almost non-existent; all postulates about the inborn wickedness of the child—its aggressive and sadistic 'instincts'—have been abandoned, sometimes by rationalization, sometimes merely by default. In American psychoanalytical thinking, the child is born faultless, a *tabula rasa*, and any defects which subsequently develop are the fault of uncontrollable circumstances. . . ." To the American sensibility, the Freudian version of the doctrine of Original Sin appears to be no less distasteful than the Christian.

Finally, there is the belief that because our nature is fundamentally good, we have only to act naturally in order to act virtuously. "They define virtue," More wrote of his Utopians, "as living according to nature," and the same equation is apparent in the social norms I dis-

cussed in Chapter Three, namely the distinctively American insistence on openness and spontaneity. For in a culture like Europe which still believes in the Fall of Man, nature has to be redeemed by art and guilt demands concealment. But in a culture like America which believes in human innocence, art can serve only to corrupt nature and there is no guilt to be concealed. The pure in heart, after all, have nothing to hide from each other.

The technical term for this congeries of radically anti-Puritan ideas is Pelagianism, the heresy named after the Celtic monk who introduced it to the Roman church in the fourth century of our era. From then onwards it has been the object of virulent attacks by European theologians ranging from St. Augustine and St. Bernard of Clairvaux to Martin Luther and John Calvin. To the Old World, with its long history of human folly and wickedness, the teachings of Pelagius have always seemed impossibly optimistic. To the New World, however, they have proved to be immensely appealing, and it is not hard, I think, to see why. Indeed, the reason is suggested by their proponent's very name, which means in Latin "open sea." Pelagianism, one might say, is the heresy of human boundlessness. As such, it could hardly fail to find a home in a culture based upon the denial of every form of limit.

The spirit which thus transformed a European heresy into an American principle has been expressed most memorably in one of the late Senator Robert Kennedy's favorite sayings: "You see things; and you say 'Why?' But I dream things that never were; and I say 'Why not?' " They are stirring words, and for me at least they encapsulate the American attitude to life. But in fact they were written by a European, George Bernard Shaw, who put them in the mouth of one of the central characters in his panoramic drama *Back to Methuselah* (1921), the opening scene of which takes place in the garden of Eden. It is a measure, perhaps, of the difference between the American and the European sensibilities that the character to whom Shaw gave his visionary question was the serpent.

Second Childhood

Translated from theological into psychological terms, the process of immigration becomes a return not to the garden of Eden but to the state of infancy. In Franz Kafka's novel *Amerika* (1927), the image of rebirth is thus taken quite literally, and the experience of settling in this country is portrayed as a second childhood. Karl Rossman, the book's protagonist, is a mature young man of sixteen or so who has come to America in order to escape the disgrace of having fathered an illegitimate child by his parents' maidservant. But as soon as he reaches New

York, he begins to behave as if he were a child himself. For instance, he is constantly losing things—his umbrella, his precious box of mementoes, his hat, and on at least two occasions himself. Worse still, everyone he meets in America treats him like a child. At a dinner party in his Uncle Jacob's house nobody takes the slightest notice of him, and he is left "silently to occupy himself with his food, as if he were a child who had merely to sit up straight and empty his plate." At another dinner party, this time at the home of one of his uncle's friends, his host takes him on his knees "although as a rule Karl felt much too grown up for such treatment."

Such treatment, though, merely reflects the fact that in a very real sense Karl *has* regressed to childhood. He is "an American so new and untried" that he is virtually helpless to cope with the unfamiliar environment in which he suddenly finds himself. "The first days of a European in America," his uncle explains to him, "might be likened to a rebirth, and though Karl was not to worry about it unduly, since one got used to things here more quickly than an infant coming into the world from the other side, yet he must keep in mind that first judgments were always unreliable." Like a child he thus has to learn a new language, and his acceptability in adult society appears to depend in large measure upon how quickly he masters it. "The better Karl's English became," we are informed, "the greater inclination his uncle showed to introduce him to his friends." Like a child, too, he is frequently overwhelmed by the sheer size of everything he encounters. As the ship carrying him to New York passes the Statue of Liberty, he murmurs to himself "so high," and once he actually lands in this country his sense of scale is assaulted on all sides. His uncle's car is "towering." His uncle's friend Mr. Pollunder lives in a house which is "larger and taller than a country house designed for only one family has any need to be." The figure of another of his uncle's friends, Mr. Green, is "gigantic," while the cigar he carries is "of a thickness which Karl's father in Austria . . . had probably never seen with his own eyes." Even the newspapers strike him as being "enormous."

The most complete rendering of this experience, however, is to be found in the concluding chapters of the novel when Karl finds himself in the Great Nature Theater of Oklahoma, Kafka's emblem for America as a whole. Upon seeing it for the first time Karl "realized that it was all on a much larger scale than he could have conceived possible." "It's the biggest theater in the world," he learns from his fiancée shortly afterwards. "I haven't seen it yet myself," she continues, "but some of the girls here, who have been in Oklahoma already, say that there are almost no limits to it." So large is it, indeed, that it can apparently accommodate an unlimited number of applicants. "Everyone is welcome" announce the placards at the entrance. "Our Theater can find employment for everyone, a place for everyone." As de Crèvecoeur remarked in the essay I quoted earlier, "There is room for everyone in America."

In temporal terms, too, Karl perceives his new home from an essentially childlike point of view, for it appears to him that everything in America is moving at tremendous speed. In Uncle Jacob's office, for instance, "there was a perpetual tumult of people rushing hither and thither. Nobody said good day, greetings were omitted, each man fell into step behind anyone who was going the same way, keeping his eyes on the floor, over which he was set on advancing as quickly as he could, or giving a hurried glance at a word or figure here and there on the papers he held in his hand, which fluttered with the wind of his progress." The theater-goers Karl sees on the street outside "hurried along with flying steps or drove in vehicles at the utmost possible speed." The elevators in the hotel where Karl eventually finds employment as a lift-boy fly up and down like hysterical yo-yos. The head porter's office is full of "people all working at top speed and without an eye for anything unconnected with their work." And all the time the traffic on the roads leading into and out of New York careers past in a demented frenzy of speed. One could hardly wish, I think, for a better image of the European's initial response to the bewildering energy and size of America, a child's-eye view of the grown-up world: immense, hectic, incomprehensible—exhilarating and terrifying at the same time.

But perhaps the most interesting thing of all about this novel is the way it ends—or rather the way it doesn't end. For like many of his other works, Kafka's *Amerika* is unfinished. In a brief postscript his friend Max Brod informs us that "the incomplete chapter about the Nature Theater of Oklahoma . . . was intended to be the concluding chapter of the work, and should end on a note of reconciliation. In enigmatic language Kafka used to hint smilingly that within this 'almost limitless' theater his young hero was going to find again a profession, a stand-by, his freedom, even his old home and his parents, as if by some celestial witchery." In this particular instance, however, it is singularly appropriate that the novel should not have been concluded. For any conclusion, even a utopian one, is the narrative embodiment of limit, the pillars of Hercules beyond which the story is not permitted to proceed. As Aristotle stated in his *Poetics*, an ending is "that which itself naturally follows some other thing . . . but has nothing following it." If Kafka was to remain true to his vision of America, it is hard to see how he could ever have imposed such a terminal event upon his novel. How could a book about infinite possibilities ever achieve completion without deny-

Rain, Steam, Speed by Joseph Turner.

ing its own fundamental nature? How could any finite destination satisfy a hero who has come to exemplify the interminable American quest for success?

Instead, Kafka leaves us with an image of a continuing journey across an apparently limitless landscape. The last paragraph of the novel reads:

> The first day they traveled through a high range of mountains. Masses of blue-black rock rose in sheer wedges to the railway line; even craning one's neck out of the window, one could not see their summits: narrow, gloomy, jagged valleys opened out and one tried to follow with a pointing finger the direction in which they lost themselves; broad mountain streams appeared, rolling in great waves down on to the foothills and drawing with them a thousand foaming wavelets, plunging underneath the bridges over which the train rushed; and they were so near that the breath of coldness rising from them chilled the skin of one's face.

Indefinite extension in space has found its equivalent in indefinite extension in time, and the novel dissolves in a shimmering haze of undefined possibilities. One can begin to understand, I think, why Kafka subtitled the novel *The Man Who Was Lost Sight Of*. Like the typical American hero that he has by now become, Karl Rossman, when we last see him, is on his way somewhere else, traveling hopefully towards a destination at which he will never arrive.

Dise figur anzaigt vns das volck vnd insel die gefunden ist durch den cristenlichen künig zů Portugal oder von seinen vnderthonen. Die leüt sind also nacket hübsch braun wolgestalt von leib ir h balß arm scham füß frawen vnd mann ain wenig mit federn bedeckt. Auch haben die mann in iren angesichtē vnd brust vil edel gestain. Es hat auch nyemantz nichts sunder sind alle ding ge Vnd die mann habend weyber welche in gefallen es sey můter schwester oder freündt darinn haben sy nit vnderschayd. Sy streyten auch mit ainander. Sy essen auch ainander selbs die ersch w tden vnd hencken das selbig flaisch in den rauch. Sy werden alt hundert vnd fünfftzig iar. Vnd hat ain kain regiment.

The People of the Islands Recently Discovered, anonymous, German.

CHAPTER FIVE

THE IGNOBLE SAVAGE

So as marvel you not at the thin population of America, nor at the rudeness and ignorance of the people, for you must account your inhabitants of America as a young people, younger a thousand years at the least than the rest of the world.

Sir Francis Bacon, *The New Atlantis*, 1627

THE RELATIONSHIP between the inhabitants of the Old World and the New has been fraught with mutual misunderstandings from the very moment they first encountered each other in 1492. The natives of Hispaniola, wrote Columbus, "were very firmly convinced that I, with these ships and men, came from the heavens, and in this belief they everywhere received me after they had mastered their fear. At present, those I bring with me are still of the opinion that I come from Heaven, for all the intercourse which they have had with me. They were the first to announce this wherever I went, and the others went running from house to house and to the neighboring towns, with loud cries of, 'Come. Come. See the men from Heaven.'" The explorers in turn were convinced that the men and women they had "discovered" were noble savages, free of the aggressiveness, acquisitiveness, and hypocrisy which tainted human nature in Europe. The people, Columbus declared, "have no iron or steel or weapons, nor are they fitted to use them. This is not because they are not well built and of handsome stature but because they are marvelously timorous. . . . They are so guileless and so generous with all that they possess that no one would believe it who has not seen it. They refuse nothing that they possess, . . . and display as much love as if they would give their hearts." Both parties were swiftly disillusioned. Columbus' men behaved so badly on Hispaniola that within a relatively short time they came to be regarded by the native population as devils rather than gods. On their side, the Tainos soon revealed that they were capable of acting quite as treacherously and ferociously as their European persecutors. The heavenly visitors and the noble savages turned out to be considerably less heavenly and less noble than they had first appeared to each other.

The image of *homo Americanus* that gradually evolved in the European imagination over the next few centuries seems to me to be an amalgam of the four basic elements involved in this seminal encounter between the Old World and the New: it incorporates, that is to say, not only the positive and the negative characteristics originally attributed to the indigenous population of America but also the positive and the negative characteristics subsequently associated with the early European explorers and settlers.

Unfallen Human Nature

To begin with the Indians, their primary quality was thought by most of the explorers to be their innocence. If the New World was another Eden, it was only natural, after all, that it should be inhabited by unfallen men and women who wore no clothes and felt no shame. "All of both sexes go about naked," observed Vespucci in his pamphlet *The New World* (1503), "and just as they spring from their mothers' wombs so they go unto death." As in the case of Adam and Eve, moreover, their physical nakedness symbolized their moral and sexual purity, for according to such influential writers as Peter Martyr and Montaigne, the American natives led lives of uncorrupted simplicity and virtue. According to the latter, indeed, they exemplified the nobility of which humanity was capable so long as it remained unsullied by the vices of European civilization. "These nations," he declared in his essay *On Cannibals*, "then seem to me to be so far barbarous as having received but very little form and fashion from art and human invention, and being consequently not much remote from their original simplicity. The laws of nature govern them still, not as yet much vitiated with any mixture of ours; nay, in such purity that I am sometimes troubled we were no sooner acquainted with these people, and that they were not discovered in those better times when there were men much more

Les Nouvelles Indes after Alexandre–François Desportes, Gobelins Tapestry Factory.

able to judge of them than we are." In the second Eden across the Atlantic, the fruit of the tree of knowledge was still untasted.

Implicit in many Renaissance accounts of the Indians' innocence is the metaphor we encountered in Kafka's rendering of the immigrant experience: the metaphor of childhood. American man, Montaigne remarked in his essay *On Coaches* (1588), is "so new and infantile that he is yet to learn his *ABCs*. It is not yet full fifty years that he knew neither letters nor weights nor measures, nor apparel nor corn nor vines; but was all naked, simply-pure in Nature's lap, and lived but with such means and food as his mother-nurse afforded him." He resembled a child most strikingly, it seemed to the explorers, in his readiness to trust and befriend the strangers who had discovered him. "We found the people," Philip Amadas and Arthur Barlow informed Sir Walter Raleigh, "most gentle, loving and faithful, void of all guile and treason, and such as live after the manner of the golden age." The natives of California, echoed Francis Fletcher in *The World Encompassed* (1628), are "a people of a tractable, free, and loving nature, without guile or treachery."

As a result, the inhabitants of the New World were an easy prey to the guile and treachery of their visitors. Unaware of the value which was placed upon gold and silver in Europe, they readily offered considerable amounts of both metals in return for mere trinkets. "They are content with whatever trifle of whatever kind that may be given to them," wrote Columbus, "whether it be of value or valueless. I forbade that they should be given things so worthless as fragments of broken crockery, scraps of broken glass and lace tips, although when they were able to get them, they fancied that they possessed the best jewel in the world. So it was found that for a thong a sailor received gold to the weight of two and a half castellanos, and others received much more for other things which were worth less." But even this highly profitable bartering was not enough to satisfy Columbus' crew. According to the great sixteenth-century Spanish historian Bartolomé de las Casas, "The Indians were so liberal and the Spaniards so greedy and unrestrained, it was not enough for them that for a lace end and even for a bit of glass and of earthenware and for other things of no value the Indians would give them whatever they desired, but without giving anything to them they wished to have and take everything." As Montaigne insisted later in the century, it was the "adults" from Europe who taught the "children" of the New World how to cheat and betray.

Unredeemed Human Nature

From the very beginning, however, there was another side to the image of *homo Americanus* as he appeared in the travel literature of the Renaissance. For it was first rumored and then confirmed that certain tribes in the West Indies and South America transgressed one of the most deep-seated of all human taboos; they practiced cannibalism. In his letter to Santangel, Columbus stated that he had heard of a tribe called the Caribes "who are regarded in all the islands as very fierce and who eat human flesh." Vespucci, whose view of the Indians was consistently more hostile than Columbus', actually claimed to have encountered the phenomenon at first hand. "They eat one another," he reported in *The New World*, "the victors the vanquished, and among other kinds of meat, human flesh is a common article of diet with them. . . . I likewise saw salted human flesh suspended from beams between the houses, just as with us it is the custom to hang bacon and pork. . . . We endeavored to the extent of our power to persuade them to desist from these depraved customs, and they did promise us that they would leave off."

Nor was this the only respect, Vespucci declared in his *Four Voyages*, in which their manner of living was "barbarous." They urinated wherever and whenever the mood took them, they were extremely libidinous and practiced polygamy, and they treated their sick with a callousness that would have been unthinkable in most European countries. Those who fell ill were simply left out in the wilderness for four to six days with a small supply of food and drink. If they survived the ordeal, they were accepted back into the tribe. If they didn't, there was no need to worry about them any further.

As the existence of such practices revealed, the natives of America were not Christians, and this fact provided successive generations of European explorers and settlers with a perfect motive for taking possession of the New World: they were liberating its inhabitants from the tyranny of pagan ignorance. "What a great, meritorious deed it were," wrote Sir Thomas More's brother-in-law John Rastell in *The Interlude of the Four Elements* (1512-19):

> To have the people instructed
> To live more virtuously,
> And to learn to know of men the manner,
> And also to know God their Maker,
> Which as yet live all beastly;
> For they neither know God nor the devil,
> Nor never heard tell of heaven nor hell,
> Writing nor other scripture;
> But yet, in the stead of God almighty

Cannibal Scene, anonymous, after Hans Staden. (From Théodor de Bry's *America, Part III*.)

> They honor the sun for his great light,
> For that doth them great pleasure.

Territorial conquest could thus be sanctioned by the opportunities it opened up for religious conversion, and in promotional works ranging from the *Journal* of Christopher Columbus to Richard Hakluyt's *Discourse of Western Planting* (1584), one finds the material and spiritual justifications for colonization appearing, often somewhat uneasily, side by side. "Your Highnesses should resolve," Columbus wrote to Ferdinand and Isabella, "to make them Christians, for I believe that, if you begin, in a little while you will achieve the conversion of a great number of peoples to our holy faith, with the acquisition of great lordships and riches and all of their inhabitants for Spain."

The Church, needless to say, was happy to cooperate in this great venture. Frustrated by Turkish expansion in the East, it now had an ideal outlet for its evangelical energies in the West. In 1537 Pope Paul III issued the famous bull *Sublimis Deus* declaring that the population of America was both capable and desirous of receiving the Catholic faith, and despite the doubts raised by such influential figures as Juan Ginés de Sepúlveda and Gonzalo Fernández de Oviedo concerning the spiritual and intellectual status of the Indians, a stream of European divines crossed the Atlantic in search of new converts. As the opening scene of Evelyn Waugh's *The Loved One* suggests, the Old World has never lost this long-cherished conviction that it has been appointed by Providence to civilize and enlighten the benighted inhabitants of the New. Secure in their unshakable belief in the cultural superiority of Europe, Dennis Barlow and Sir Frank Hinsley, like so many of their Renaissance predecessors, really do think of themselves as missionaries in a barbarous land, bearers of wisdom, grace, and learning to a savage people.

Brave Heroic Minds

Which brings me to the second pair of constituents in the European image of American man, namely the conflicting perceptions that developed of the colonists themselves. The tone of the earliest descriptions of these intrepid spirits is suggested by the concluding stanza of a poem written by a certain Captain Bingham in commendation of Sir George Peckam's treatise, *A True Report of the Late Discoveries of the New Found Lands* (1583):

> Then launch, ye noble youths, into the main;
> No lurking perils lie amid the way;
> Your travail shall return you treble gain,

And make your names renowned another day.
For valiant minds through twenty seas will roam
And fish for luck, while sluggards lie at home.

In a similar vein Sir Richard Grenville Sr., the father of the leader of the ill-fated Virginian expedition of 1585, declared in a poem in praise of seafaring men:

Who seeks the way to win renown
Or flies with wings of high desire;
Who seeks to wear the laurel crown,
Or hath the mind that would aspire:
Tell him his native soil eschew,
Tell him go range and seek anew.

To pass the seas some think a toil,
Some think it strange abroad to roam,
Some think it grief to leave their soil,
Their parents, kinsfolk and their home;
Think so who list, I like it not,
I must abroad to try my lot.

And Michael Drayton, anxious to drum up volunteers for the British colony in Virginia, began his ode "To the Virginian Voyage" (1606) as follows:

You brave, heroic minds
Worthy your country's name,
That honor still pursue,
Go and subdue,
Whilst loitering hinds
Lurk here at home for shame.

Sentiments such as these were perhaps only natural in the great age of exploration, but they recur in European commentaries on the American character written long after that initial burst of enthusiasm was over. In the nineteenth century, for example, Charles Dickens remarked in his *American Notes* that "it is a singular though very natural feature in the society of these distant settlements, that it is mainly composed of adventurous persons in the prime of life." Early in our own century George Santayana observed that "the discovery of the new world exercised a sort of selection among the inhabitants of Europe. . . . The fortunate, the deeply rooted, and the lazy remained at home; the wilder instincts or dissatisfaction of others tempted them beyond the horizon. The American is accordingly the most adventurous, or the descendant of the most adventurous, of Europeans." And still more recently, the British historian J.H. Elliott has suggested in *The Old World and the New* (1970) that "if, as seems plausible, [those who emigrated to America] were above average in intelligence and ability, there could have been some loss in the genetic quality of the population [of Europe] as a whole" as a result of their departure. Whether they are perceived as colonists, settlers, emigrants, or all three rolled into one, those who journeyed to the New World are consistently portrayed by European writers as being more ambitious, more energetic, and more daring than those who stayed behind in the Old. In his heroic refusal "to renounce the quest / Of what may in the sun's path be assayed," Dante's Ulysses might well have been their prototype.

The Outcasts of Europe

A very different image of the planters, as they were called in the Renaissance, emerges from the writings of several other famous proponents of the colonization of America. The population of England, they argued, had grown so dramatically in the fifteenth and sixteenth centuries that the country was bursting at the seams. The vast continent across the Atlantic, on the contrary, was still only sparsely inhabited, and as such it offered precisely the kind of *lebensraum* that the nation so desperately needed. Just as a stream discharges its waters into the ocean, wrote the slave-trader John Hawkins in 1583,

> So England, that is pestered now and choked through want of
>   ground,
> Shall find a soil where room enough and profit doth abound.
> The Romans, when the number of their people grew so great
> As neither wars could waste nor Rome suffice them for a seat,
> They led them forth by swarming troops to foreign lands amain
>   [in haste],
> And founded divers colonies unto the Roman reign. . . .
>
> But neither Rome nor Athens nor the rest were never pestered so
> As England, where no room remains her dwellers to bestow,
> But shuffled in such pinching bonds that very breath doth lack,
> And for the want of place they crawl one o'er another's back.
> How nobly, then, shall they provide that for redress herein,
> With ready hand and open purse this action doth begin;
> Whence glory to the name of God and country's good shall spring.

By solving the problem of overpopulation, moreover, the acquisition of new territory in America would simultaneously solve the associated problems of unemployment and the social unrest that came in its train.

For as Raphael Hythloday had observed in Book I of *Utopia*, one of the principal reasons for the high crime rate in sixteenth-century England was the large number of people living in enforced idleness. If they could be put to work across the Atlantic, Richard Hakluyt concluded in his *Discourse of Western Planting*, then not only would their native land be relieved of a constant source of trouble; it would profit handsomely from their labors as well. The Spanish and the Portuguese, he wrote,

> by these their new discoveries have so many ways to set [the unemployed] on work, as they rather lack men than means to employ them. But we, for all the statutes that hitherto can be devised, and the sharp execution of the same in punishing idle and lazy persons, for want of sufficient occasion of honest employment cannot deliver our commonwealth from multitudes of loiterers and idle vagabonds ... which, having no way to be set on work, be either mutinous and seek alteration in the state, or at least very burdensome to the commonwealth, and often fall to pilfering and thieving and other lewdness, whereby all the prisons of the land are daily pestered and stuffed full of them. ... Whereas if this voyage were put in execution, these petty thieves might be condemned for certain years in the western parts.

Or as John Donne put it in a sermon he preached to the Honorable Company of the Virginia Plantation in 1622, the establishment of a thriving colony in North America might serve to "redeem many a wretch from the jaws of death, from the hands of the executioner." "It shall sweep your streets," he promised his audience, "and wash your doors from idle persons, and the children of idle persons, and employ them; and truly, if the country were but such a Bridewell [a well-known London prison] to force idle persons to work, it had a good use."

Besides providing an alternative explanation for the prevalence of the so-called Protestant work ethic in this country, such passages reveal that America was perceived by many Renaissance Englishmen either as an enormous public works project designed to occupy the energies of the unemployed or as a vast penal colony in which the nation's malcontents, criminals, dissenters, and heretics could conveniently be confined at a safe distance from civilized society. It is no accident, perhaps, that Sir Thomas More's prophetic vision of America in Book II of *Utopia* should resemble nothing so much as the ideal prison system described by Raphael Hythloday in Book I of the same work.

The disadvantages of the policy advocated by Hakluyt and Donne appeared very early in the history of European settlements in the New

World. At the beginning of the sixteenth century Peter Martyr complained bitterly that the men whom Columbus took with him on his second voyage "were for the most part undisciplined, unscrupulous vagabonds, who only employed their ingenuity in gratifying their appetites. Incapable of moderation in their acts of injustice, they carried off the women of the islanders under the very eyes of their brothers and husbands; given over to violence and thievery, they profoundly vexed the natives." And the same problem afflicted the first English attempts at colonization in North America almost a century later. A.L. Rowse, for instance, has argued persuasively that one of the chief reasons for the failure of the Roanoke expedition was the nature of the settlers who undertook it. "The first Virginian voyages," he writes, "transported the flotsam and jetsam of humanity. Often lazy, they had to be threatened with starvation to work." By the time Sir Francis Bacon published his essay *Of Plantations* (1625), there was ample evidence to support his arguments against treating the New World as a European penitentiary. "It is a shameful and unblessed thing," he declared, "to take the scum of people and wicked condemned men to be the people with whom you plant; and not only so, but it spoileth the plantation, for they will ever live like rogues, and not fall to work, but be lazy, and do mischief, and spend victuals, and be quickly weary, and then certify over to their country to the discredit of the plantation."

Despite his protests, however, the practice continued throughout the seventeenth century. After 1660 criminals under sentence of death were given the alternative of transportation to America, and in 1685 alone the infamous Judge Jeffreys ordered more than one thousand of them to be shipped across the Atlantic. In the years that followed, it has been estimated, more than fifty thousand common criminals were condemned to hard labor in the colonies. Once again Sir Thomas More's description of Utopia had turned out to be prophetic. "Their bondmen," he wrote of the Utopians, "are either their own citizens who have been sentenced to bondage for some crime, or men of other nations who have been condemned to death. The Utopians buy these men at a low price, or more often obtain them free of charge and bring them home. All kinds of bondmen are kept constantly at work and are always chained." To the men and women of the seventeenth century it must have seemed that a significant proportion of the white as well as the black population of America first arrived in their adopted country in chains.

The image of the immigrant as an actual or potential jailbird is still visible, I think, in several nineteenth-century accounts of the United States, notably in Charles Dickens' *American Notes* and *Martin Chuzzlewit*. Page after page of the former is devoted to American "houses of correction," as Dickens called them, and if their actual number were in proportion to their prominence in his commentary, we might well conclude that in 1842 America consisted largely of jails, asylums, and poorhouses. But it is in *Martin Chuzzlewit* that the penal theme emerges most clearly. As the ship carrying Martin and his companions to the New World arrives in New York harbor, "an English gentleman who was strongly suspected of having run away from a bank with something in his possession belonging to its strong-box besides the key, grew eloquent upon the subject of the rights of man and hummed the Marseillaise Hymn constantly." And indeed the entire country subsequently proves to be populated by rogues, confidence men, thieves, and swindlers. Their apotheosis is the terrifying figure whom Martin encounters in the swamps of Eden, Mr. Chollop:

> Mr. Chollop was, of course, one of the most remarkable men in the country; but he really was a notorious person besides. He was usually described by his friends in the South and West as "a splendid sample of our native raw material, sir," and was much esteemed for his devotion to rational Liberty; for the better propagation whereof he usually carried a brace of revolving pistols in his coat pocket, with seven barrels apiece. He also carried amongst other trinkets, a swordstick, which he called his "Tickler"; and a great knife, which (for he was a man of a pleasant turn of humor) he called "Ripper" in allusion to its usefulness as a means of ventilating the stomach of any adversary in a close contest. He had used these weapons with distinguished effect in several instances, all duly chronicled in the newspapers; and was greatly beloved for the gallant manner in which he had "jobbed out" the eye of one gentleman, as he was in the act of knocking at his own street-door.
>
> Mr. Chollop was a man of a roving disposition; and, in any less advanced community, might have been mistaken for a violent vagabond. But his fine qualities being perfectly understood and appreciated in those regions where his lot was cast, and where he had many kindred spirits to consort with, he may be regarded as having been born under a fortunate star, which is not always the case with a man so much before the age in which he lives.

Drayton's "brave heroic minds" have turned into a society of barbarians.

An Innocent Abroad

All four of the images I have so far treated in isolation merge together in the protagonist of Graham Greene's controversial novel *The Quiet American* (1955). Narrated by Thomas Fowler, a world-weary British war correspondent reporting the struggle between the French and the Vietminh in the early 1950s, it describes the adventures of Alden Pyle, a young Harvard graduate who arrives in Vietnam equipped with inexhaustible energy, impenetrable seriousness, and a theory (acquired from one of his political textbooks) that a Third Force is required to restore stable government in the embattled country. His energy and seriousness soon endear him to Fowler's Vietnamese mistress, Phuong, to whom he becomes engaged. His political theory has less romantic consequences. Despite Fowler's warnings, he supplies large quantities of a powerful explosive called Diolacton to a treacherous Vietnamese warlord, General Thé, in the hope of establishing him as ruler, independent of the French and the Vietminh. The result is a bungled attempt to sabotage a military parade; the parade is canceled, but the time-bombs General Thé's men have planted go off anyway, killing and maiming a large number of civilians. Outraged by Pyle's evident indifference to the suffering he has caused, Fowler reluctantly agrees to set him up for what he would like to believe is an interview with the Vietminh but what he fully realizes will be an assassination. He arranges to meet Pyle at a specified time in a certain Saigon restaurant; Pyle keeps the appointment and is duly murdered. Phuong, apparently untouched by his death, returns to live with Fowler, who is free to marry her now that his English wife has consented to divorce him.

Even this bare outline of the story may be sufficient to suggest why *The Quiet American* was accorded anything but a quiet reception when it first appeared in the United States. "This man's caricature of the American abroad" was the title of one review. "To get rave reviews [presumably in Europe] write an anti-U.S. novel" advised another. Greene was repeatedly accused of embodying in Alden Pyle all that he most disliked about this country and using Thomas Fowler as a stick to beat him with. The deepening American involvement in Southeast Asia that took place after the book was published inevitably served to reinforce this view in many quarters, with the result that *The Quiet American* is now widely regarded as a thinly disguised critique of American foreign policy.

So offensive was the novel to the sensibilities of a Hollywood film-producer, indeed, that he felt compelled to make a motion picture version in which all the faults that the reviewers had found in the novel were vigorously remedied. Quite apart from the usual concessions to what passed for good taste in the cinema of the 1950s—for example, the thriving brothel in which many of the book's central episodes take place was rehabilitated as a relatively genteel restaurant—the presumed anti-American bias of the plot was corrected by the revelation that Alden Pyle, played by war hero Audie Murphy, was in fact the innocent victim of a Communist conspiracy. Fowler, it turns out in the film, was goaded by jealousy into being the dupe of the Vietminh. There is no such explosive as Diolacton, Fowler learns from a contemptuous French police inspector; he has been taken in by crudely manufactured evidence against his innocent young rival. Not surprisingly, therefore, Phuong, far from returning to marry her aging British protector, reproaches him bitterly for causing the death of her one true love, Alden Pyle. Thus the blindfold that Justice had so obstinately worn in Greene's original story is triumphantly removed, and a real pro-American prejudice is substituted for an illusory anti-American one.

I say "illusory" because I do not believe that Fowler's (or Greene's) attitude to Alden Pyle is nearly as uncomplicated as the first American reviewers obviously assumed. It seems to me, on the contrary, that both the narrator and the author have very mixed feelings about "the quiet American," and that they do so because they are capable of perceiving in him virtually all the positive as well as the negative aspects of the American character that I have attempted to identify above. The book's final judgment upon its protagonist, I would like to suggest, is very finely balanced indeed.

To begin with, Pyle is quite as free of guile and malice as the noble savages whom the first explorers believed they had found. When he falls in love with Fowler's mistress, for instance, he not only insists on informing his rival that he proposes to marry her; he scrupulously avoids taking advantage of the fact that the older man is already married. The kind of deception in which virtually every other character in the book engages at one time or another is clearly beyond him. On the one occasion that he attempts a small lie, Fowler notes wryly that "he was one of the most inefficient liars I have ever known—it was an art he had obviously never practised."

His lack of malice is equally striking. Alden Pyle wishes ill to no one, not even to the man who threatens to obstruct his love affair with Phuong. Although he has everything to gain from leaving his wounded rival behind to die when the two of them are trapped out in the rice paddies by the Vietminh, Pyle risks his own life to drag Fowler to safety. "If it had been you," the latter comments ungratefully as he reflects back on the incident later, "I'd have left you." Indeed, in view of the way in which most of the other characters treat him, "lack of malice" hardly seems to do justice to Pyle's indefatigable benevolence. Fowler informs us early in the novel that "he was determined to do good—I learnt that very soon—to do good, not to any individual person but to a country, a continent, a world," and as it turns out even Pyle's most destructive actions are motivated by good will. A comment Fowler makes about him not long after his death could well be his epitaph. "I never knew a man," Fowler confesses, "who had better motives for all the trouble he caused."

At times, nevertheless, Pyle is capable of behaving with a degree of cruelty and inhumanity reminiscent of the barbarous cannibals whom the explorers encountered in several parts of the New World. In the pivotal scene of the novel, for instance, after witnessing at first hand the terrible suffering he has indirectly brought about by supplying General Thé with explosives, he looks down at the blood a dying child has spattered on his shoes and murmurs, "I must get them cleaned before I see the Minister." The appalling callousness of that remark, the memory of which haunts Fowler throughout the rest of the book, reveals the tragic inability of the innocent to comprehend the suffering they may unintentionally inflict upon their fellow human beings. "He was as incapable of imagining pain or danger to himself," Fowler observes, "as he was incapable of conceiving the pain he might cause others." Because he means no harm, he is blind to the fact that he may be doing some. As Fowler puts it, "he was impregnably armored by his good intentions."

Like the early explorers and settlers, on the other hand, Pyle is also characterized by the sheer amount of energy, courage, and personal engagement he brings to bear upon the world in which he finds himself. The intensity of his commitment is particularly evident if we compare it, as Greene invites us to, with the detachment of his European antagonist. "You can rule me out," exclaims Fowler when he is accused of complicity in Pyle's death. "I'm not involved. Not involved. . . . It had been an article of my creed. The human condition being what it was, let them fight, let them love, let them murder, I would not be involved. My fellow journalists called themselves correspondents; I preferred the title of reporter. I wrote what I saw: I took no action—even an opinion is a kind of action." I find it hard to believe that this position is being held up for our admiration, for the inadequacy of Fowler's creed is one of the book's major themes. "Sooner or later," he is reminded by an agent of the Vietminh, "one has to take sides. If one is to remain human." Pyle takes sides with a vengeance, albeit the wrong ones. He

The Spanish Treatment of Fugitive Black Slaves. (From Théodor de Bry's *America*, Part V.)

is willing to commit himself, however naively, to an opinion or a course of action. As Fowler admits with more than a trace of envy, "Pyle believed in being involved."

Unfortunately, his involvement is so uncompromising that he eventually comes to be regarded by the other characters in the novel in much the same way as the early colonists were regarded by many of their sixteenth- and seventeenth-century contemporaries, namely as a danger to civilized human society. Not, of course, that he is either a thief or a vagabond. He resembles, rather, those political and religious dissidents who, in Hakluyt's words, sought "alteration in the state." Like the Puritans in particular, he is absolutely convinced of the rectitude of his own beliefs and insists on attempting to impose them on his fellow men. Like the Puritans, too, he has a sacred text (in his case *The Advance of Red China* by a third-rate political scientist named York Harding), which he treats with unquestioning reverence. "He was very, very serious," Fowler notes early in their relationship. "I was to learn later that he had an enormous respect for what he called serious writers. That term excluded novelists, poets and dramatists unless they had what he called a contemporary theme, and even then it was better to read the straight stuff as you got it from York." Pyle, in his own quiet way, is a zealot, a mild-mannered fanatic whose unwavering moral earnestness and inflexible adherence to principle would have found a congenial home in colonial New England.

In his refusal to accommodate his high-minded ideals to the imperfections of the real world he reminds me still more, however, of the very first incarnation of the American spirit in the literature of Europe: Raphael Hythloday, the discoverer of Utopia. There is the same evangelical intensity, the same longing to reform society, the same disregard for his own personal welfare. The only difference, and it is a crucial one, is that whereas Hythloday believed with Plato that "a wise man will not meddle in affairs of state," Alden Pyle cannot resist attempting to translate his political theories into practice. For Greene's quiet American is an absolutist at large in what his creator evidently believes to be a universe capable of only relative improvements, a Raphael Hythloday determined to enforce his philosophy upon the kind of world Sir Thomas More actually lived in.

This extraordinary combination of innocence and cruelty, commitment and intolerance, is at least partially attributable to what for Thomas Fowler is clearly Alden Pyle's most striking single characteristic, his youthfulness. "Americans are boys," announced Salvador de Madariaga in an essay published by *Harper's Monthly Magazine* in 1928, and Greene's novel might have been written to illustrate his thesis.

When he gave Pyle his first briefing, Fowler recalls, "he watched me intently like a prize pupil," and throughout the rest of the book the Harvard graduate is compared over and over again with a schoolboy. Trapped in a watchtower by the Vietminh, " 'What happens next?' Pyle asked, like a schoolboy watching a demonstration in a laboratory." Punting down to Phat Diem through the enemy lines, he had acted, Fowler recalls later, "with the caution of a hero in a boy's adventure story, proud of his caution like a Scout's badge and quite unaware of the absurdity and improbability of his adventure." In his embarrassment over discussing his relationship with Phuong, he "gave a lost gesture, like a boy put up to speak at some school function, who cannot find the grown-up words." And as he explained to Fowler how he had rebuked General Thé for killing and maiming innocent civilians, he "spoke like the captain of a school-team who has found one of his boys breaking training." In Fowler's eyes at least, Pyle never grew up. Unaware of the complexities and ambiguities of human action which the older man perceives with such agonizing clarity, he blunders through the novel like a happy child, not so much a bull in a china shop as a frisky, wide-eyed calf.

This explains, I believe, why Fowler has such deeply ambivalent feelings about him. Weighing Pyle's "youth and hope and seriousness" against his own "age and despair," the Englishman is painfully aware that the former qualities are the more attractive. "All the time that his innocence had angered me," he confesses at one point, "some judge within myself had summed up in his favor, had compared his idealism, his half-baked ideas founded on the works of York Harding with my cynicism. Oh I was right about the facts, but wasn't he right too to be young and mistaken, and wasn't he perhaps a better man for a girl to spend her life with?" Living as he does in a kind of schoolboy dream totally out of touch with reality, Pyle may on occasion behave with almost inhuman callousness towards his fellow men, but at the same time he is intensely vulnerable himself. So although his only reaction to the sight of blood on his shoe is to get a shoeshine, he is quite as trusting as the child whose death he has just ignored, quite as susceptible to betrayal, whether by Phuong, Fowler, General Thé, York Harding, or even by life itself. "I was to see many times," Fowler observes, "that look of pain and disappointment touch his eyes when reality didn't match the romantic ideas he cherished, or when someone he loved or admired dropped below the impossible standard he had set."

Yet however innocent Pyle may be in this general sense, he is not innocent, Greene insists, in the more radical sense of being harmless. "God save us," says Fowler, "from the innocent and the good." We need to be saved because Alden Pyle, despite his good intentions, is the most destructive character in the book. "My first instinct," Fowler tells us, "was to protect him. It never occurred to me that there was greater need to protect myself. Innocence always calls mutely for protection when we would be so much wiser to guard ourselves against it; innocence is like a dumb leper who has lost his bell, wandering the countryside, meaning no harm." The only solution is to put the leper back in his leper colony, to confine Raphael Hythloday to his island across the Atlantic where his dreams of an ideal society can damage no one but himself. "What's the good," Fowler asks despairingly, "he'll always be innocent, you can't blame the innocent, they are always guiltless. All you can do is control them or eliminate them. Innocence is a kind of insanity."

It is the insanity, as I have been suggesting since Chapter One, of believing that the Fall never happened, of believing that men and women are invulnerable to pain, betrayal, death, and that good intentions will automatically lead to good results. So when Fowler announces that Pyle was killed "because he was too innocent to live," our response to his explanation is likely to be deeply ambiguous. On the one hand we may reluctantly agree that the naive young idealist had to be prevented from doing any more damage to a world he did not understand. On the other, we can hardly fail to acknowledge that his death is a terrible indictment of that world. For what made Alden Pyle so dangerous was not any malice or brutality on his part but rather his inability to recognize the malice and brutality of his fellow men. With his childlike trust in the theories of York Harding, the reliability of General Thé, the fidelity of Phuong, and the loyalty of Fowler, he persisted in acting as if the forbidden fruit were still untouched. And that, for many commentators, is the essence of the American tragedy, the tragedy of good will thwarted by innocence. In a world that is less than paradisal, they argue, the knowledge of good and evil is our only defense against anarchy. East of Eden, the American Adam may appear to be something less than human.

Vespucci Discovering America by Jan van der Street.

CHAPTER SIX

THE MISTRESS OF EUROPE

The American cartoonist who depicts his country, especially when it is a representation of America triumphant, or America pathetic, or America in all the dignity of her strength, always draws a woman— a woman young and graceful and beautiful, who faces the world with the serenity of confidence that comes from the knowledge that she rules. It is appropriate that Columbia is a woman. In the United States woman dominates.

Sir Alfred M. Low, *America at Home,* 1908

IN HIS INFLUENTIAL *Introduction to Cosmography* (1507), the German scientist Martin Waldseemüller proposed that the newly discovered continent across the Atlantic should be called "America" because "inasmuch as both Europe and Asia received their names from women, I see no reason why anyone should justly object to calling this part Amerige, i.e., the land of Amerigo, or America, after Amerigo, its discoverer, a man of great ability." Justly or not, many historians have in fact objected to his proposal, but that is not the point I wish to pursue here. What interests me about his statement is the shift of gender from the masculine form "Amerigo" to the feminine "America." For unless I am very much mistaken, there is more to Waldseemüller's decision than mere grammatical or mythological consistency. That America should have been conceived by the European imagination as female rather than male seems to me to say something profoundly important about the Old World's attitude to the New from the Renaissance to the present day.

The Conquest of America

Thanks largely to the influence of Petrarch, one of the most popular metaphors in European love poetry of the sixteenth and seventeenth centuries was the image of the lover as a sailor. In the *Canzoniere* itself the image had usually suggested the poet's inability to control his own amorous destiny, his sense of being adrift "among such warring winds, in a frail boat / Without a helm on the high seas." With the advent of the age of exploration, however, the metaphor took on a rather more purposeful character. Far from being a helpless mariner adrift on a turbulent ocean, the Elizabethan love poet saw himself as a heroic adventurer bound on a daring voyage of discovery. In his elegy on "Love's Progress," for instance, John Donne describes how the typical erotic navigator charts his course from "the first meridian" of the nose to the "Islands Fortunate" of the lips, and thence past "the glorious promontory" of the chin to:

> ...a boundless sea, but that thine eye
> Some island moles may scattered there descry;
> And sailing towards her India, in that way
> Shall at her fair Atlantic navel stay; ...

Sexual and maritime exploration have here become the equivalent of each other, so in another poem, "To his Mistress Going to Bed," Donne can greet his partner in the following terms:

> Oh my America, my new found land,
> My kingdom safeliest when with one man mann'd,
> My mine of precious stones, my Empiree,
> How blest am I in this discovering thee.

"Look," he accordingly instructs the sun in "The Sun Rising":

> Look, and tomorrow late, tell me
> Whether both the Indias of spice and mine
> Be where thou leftst them or lie here with me.

The India of spice in the East, which Columbus thought he had found, and the India of mine in the West, which he had actually found, coalesce in the figure of Donne's mistress. She is his America and he, by implication, is her Columbus.

Like most Renaissance analogies, this one was reversible. If making love was like a voyage of discovery, then a voyage of discovery could be like making love. As a result, the close relationship between sexual and territorial conquest soon produced in the art and literature of the period an image of the New World as a submissive and almost invariably naked young virgin waiting to yield up her charms to an older and more sophisticated lover, Europe. To take just one example, this is how the Renaissance poet and dramatist George Chapman described Guiana in a poem he wrote in honor of Sir Walter Raleigh's exploits in South America:

> Guiana, whose rich feet are mines of gold,
> Whose forehead knocks against the roof of stars,
> Stands on her tip-toes at fair England looking,
> Kissing her hand, bowing her mighty breast.

To the dismay of many Elizabethans, "fair England" did not respond very readily to such invitations, but when an English colony was eventually established on the North American continent, the very name it was given was enough to suggest the same basic metaphor. "You swore freely," wrote Richard Hakluyt to its founder and promoter, Sir Walter Raleigh, "that no terrors, no personal losses or misfortunes, could or ever would tear you from the sweet embracements of your own Virginia, that fairest of nymphs—though to many insufficiently well known— whom our most generous sovereign has given you to be your bride." And in less courtly vein a sea captain in Chapman's play *Eastward Ho* (1605) exhorted his companions to cross the Atlantic because "Virginia longs till we share the rest of her maidenhead." "A whole country of English is there," he went on to reassure them, "bred of those that were left there in seventy-nine. They have married with the Indians and make 'hem bring forth as beautiful faces as any we have in England. And therefore the Indians are so in love with them that all the treasure they have they lay at their feet." So when the modern American historian Samuel Eliot Morison writes of "those October days in 1492 when the New World gracefully yielded her virginity to the conquering Castilians," he is accurately reflecting the way in which many Renaissance authors themselves pictured the voyages of discovery. The theme that Nabokov was accused of rehearsing in *Lolita*—"old Europe debauching young America"—goes back a long way.

Vessels of Grace

As the speech of Chapman's sea captain makes clear, it was only a short step from the concept of America as a willing young virgin to the concept of American women as the predestined mistresses of European men. The female inhabitants of the New World, Vespucci proudly informed his contemporaries, "showed themselves very desirous of copulating with us Christians," and if the travel literature of the next two centuries is to be believed, the Christians were only too happy to oblige. None of the ensuing relationships was more famous than that between the Englishman John Rolfe and the Indian princess Pocahontas, whom the Virginian colonists had taken hostage while they negotiated with her father, Chief Powhatan, over the return of some of their men and supplies. When he first fell in love with her, Rolfe revealed in a letter written in 1614 to Sir Thomas Dale, the governor of Virginia, he thought that the devil was very probably responsible for his desire to link himself "with one whose education hath been rude, her manners barbarous, her generation accursed, and so discrepant in all nurture from myself." But then he heard the voice of conscience exhorting him, "Why doest thou not endeavor to make her a Christian?" In view of "her great appearance of love to me, her desire to be taught and instructed in the knowledge of God, her capableness of understanding, her aptness and willingness to receive any good impression," Rolfe was consequently moved to ask himself, "Shall I be of so untoward a disposition as to refuse to lead the blind into the right way? Shall I be so unnatural as not to give bread to the hungry? or uncharitable as not to cover the naked?" The answer was all too obvious. "I will never cease," he promised, "until I have accomplished and brought to perfection so holy a work, in which I will pray daily to God to bless me, to mine and her eternal happiness." He was motivated, he therefore asks the Governor to believe, not by "the unbridled desire of carnal affection," but rather by the Christian impulse to convert "an unbelieving creature" to the true knowledge of God.*

In this account of the considerations which prompted him to marry Pocahontas, Rolfe gave classic expression to one of the most persistent and treacherous myths ever devised about the New World by the Old, the myth that European men are irresistibly attractive to American women and have been appointed by Providence to guide them towards

---

* The girl who had turned cartwheels naked in the streets of Jamestown to entertain the colonists did not submit to Rolfe's authority quite as readily as he expected, however. When he took her to England, she shocked seventeenth-century society by entering a tavern, an incident so notorious that it found its way into Ben Jonson's play *The Staple of News*. Pocahontas, the "great King's daughter of Virginia," announces one of the characters, "Hath been in womb of tavern." But the Old World, as it has a habit of doing, had the last word. Like Daisy Miller, Pocahontas found the European climate fatal to her health, and she died in England less than a year after her husband had brought her there in 1616.

Ætatis suæ 21. Aº. 1616.

Matoaks als Rebecka daughter to the mighty Prince
Powhatan Emperour of Attanoughkomouck als Virginia
converted and baptized in the Christian faith, and
Wife to the worᵗʰ Mʳ Tho: Rolff.

Pocahontas, anonymous.

the complete sexual, moral, and spiritual fulfillment which American men have for one reason or another been unable to supply. Over the next three and a half centuries this myth appeared in a variety of different guises, but two versions of it seem to recur with particular frequency; I would like to call them the contemptuous version and the patronizing version respectively.

Fathers and Lovers

According to the contemptuous version of the myth, *femina Americana* is an empty-headed, culturally benighted, infinitely gullible child. With her "degree" in Beauticraft and her "honors thesis" on hairstyling, the heroine of Evelyn Waugh's *The Loved One* is a perfect case in point. "Aimée Thanatogenos," Waugh writes, "spoke the tongue of Los Angeles; the sparse furniture of her mind—the objects which barked the intruder's shins—had been acquired at the local High School and University; she presented herself to the world dressed and scented in obedience to the advertisements." A devotee of such self-proclaimed "experts" as Guru Brahmin, she is an easy prey to the unscrupulous British man of letters Dennis Barlow, whose sense of cultural superiority she massages at regular intervals. Dazzled by what she takes to be his infinitely greater sophistication, she offers him an ideal target at which to direct his apparently inexhaustible resources of condescension. Her only disadvantage, from Dennis' point of view, is that she refuses to conform to the traditional stereotype in one crucial particular: although she is attracted by her European mentor, she will not sleep with him.

The heroine of Nabokov's *Lolita* has no such scruples. As a matter of fact, "It was she," Humbert Humbert reveals, "who seduced me." In virtually every other respect, however, she resembles Aimée Thanatogenos very closely. Her education clearly shares the same defects—the headmistress of the school she attends explains to Humbert Humbert that "for the modern pre-adolescent child, medieval dates are of less vital value than weekend ones"—and the end product is once again a mindless, tasteless, helpless slave of the consumer society. "Mentally," confesses Humbert,

> I found her to be a disgustingly conventional little girl. Sweet hot jazz, square dancing, gooey fudge sundaes, musicals, movie magazines and so forth—these were the obvious items in her list of beloved things. . . . She believed, with a kind of celestial trust, any advertisement or advice that appeared in *Movie Love* or *Screen Land*. . . . If a roadside sign said: Visit our Gift Shop—we had to visit it, had to buy its Indian curios, dolls, copper jewelry, cactus candy. The words "novelties and

souvenirs" simply entranced her by their trochaic lilt. If some cafe sign proclaimed Icecold Drinks, she was automatically stirred, although all drinks everywhere were ice-cold. She it was to whom ads were dedicated: the ideal consumer, the subject and object of every foul poster.

As such, she offers her European admirer a pleasure which he seems to enjoy quite as much as making love to her, the pleasure of feeling immeasurably more mature, more civilized, more enlightened than she is, of playing father to her daughter.

Unequal Partners

The patronizing version of the myth is far less straightforward. At first sight, indeed, it appears to pay American women a considerable compliment, for it is based not upon their inferiority to European men but upon their superiority to American men. "There is a spaciousness in certain types of American women," declares the protagonist of Van Wyck Brooks' *The Opinions of Oliver Allston*, "that has no counterpart in the other sex; and the whole observing world has shared this feeling since the Civil War." And so, to a considerable extent, it has. Over and over again, European authors from Henry Latham, writing in 1867, to Geoffrey Gorer, writing in 1947, have paid tribute to what the latter calls "the notable ease and assurance of the American woman." Even Matthew Arnold, who found very little else to admire about the United States, was captivated by the unaffected charm of its female population. "Here we have, undoubtedly," he proclaimed, "a note of civilization"—the only one that he was able to detect in the entire culture, as it transpired. When the British journalist Douglas Woodruff asserted that "in America the women are more alive than the men," he was thus expressing a view that seems to have been held by the vast majority of European commentators who have written about the United States over the past hundred years or so.

Various explanations have been offered to account for the alleged disparity between the sexes in this country. One of the most popular is the theory originally adumbrated in Dickens' *Martin Chuzzlewit*, namely that American men are so busy making money that they have no time to improve their minds. For when Martin questions a group of them on such subjects as literature, theater, and the arts, he discovers that they are quite unable to reply. "We are a busy people, sir," he is informed, "and have no time for reading mere notions. We don't mind 'em if they come to us in newspapers along with almighty strong stuff of another sort, but darn your books." It is the women of the United States, Martin later realizes, who occupy themselves with intellectual matters—Mrs. Brick, for instance, with her passion for attending lectures, and the redoubtable Mrs. Hominy, that "masculine and towering intellect" who liked to plunge "headlong into moral philosophy at breakfast."

By the time Henry James came to write his *American Scene*, the implications of Dickens' account were widely accepted by both American and European social commentators. The "unredeemed commercialism" of the United States, James argued, had transformed the descendants of the pioneers into an undifferentiated mass of businessmen who "may never hope to be anything but business men." As a result, "the boundless, gaping void of society" (which for James was "but a rough name for all the other so numerous relations with the world he lives in that are imputable to the civilized being") was now the exclusive domain of their wives and daughters. So completely did women dominate the noncommercial aspects of life in the United States, he continued, that "the phenomenon may easily become for the spectator the sentence written largest in the American sky: when he is in search of the characteristic, what else so plays the part? The woman is two-thirds of the apparent life—which means that she is absolutely all of the social." The essential tragedy of American life, James thus concluded, was that "our vast crude democracy of trade" tended to produce men and women who were fundamentally incompatible with each other. As he wrote earlier in the same work, "from the moment the painter begins to look at American life, brush in hand, he is in danger of seeing in comparison almost nothing else in it—nothing that is so characteristic as this apparent privation, for the man, of his right kind of woman, for the woman, of her right kind of man."

For those who wish to draw it, the inference is obvious: "her right kind of man" must be socially refined, intellectually sophisticated, and non-American. In short, he must possess the very qualities which the European male has always believed distinguish him from his American counterpart. Since her own male compatriots are so "belittled and cramped by the competition of business," as Oliver Allston observed, the woman of the New World is consequently compelled to seek a partner worthy of her among the men of the Old.

Leaders of Men

Up to this point the myth has been comparatively deferential. It turns patronizing, however, as soon as the commentators begin to consider what might become of the American woman if she were left to her own devices. Paradoxically, the key to this aspect of the myth is the deference with which the men of the United States are commonly believed to treat their female superiors. "The American's profound respect for the female sex is well known," asserted the German theologian Philip Schaff in 1855, and for this reason "America is sometimes called a woman's paradise." "The reverence that is paid to women in America," agreed the English stockbroker H. Panmure Gorden some forty years later, "is outstanding." And more recently still, Salvador de Madariaga has invited us to "see the place which woman occupies in [American] life. The Boys have hoisted her on to a pedestal of admiration. Her power and privileges flow from the position she occupies as an idealized type of humanity. In her youth the inspirer, in her maturer years, the leader of men. . . . [W]oman governs America because America is a land of Boys who refuse to grow up." Deprived by his Protestant origins of the chance to worship a female divinity, the American male has committed the sin which John Milton insisted was responsible for the Fall of Man: like the protagonist of *Paradise Lost*, he has idolized his mate.

In the eyes of a good many European commentators, the results have been no less disastrous in the second Eden than they were in the first. Having reversed the traditional hierarchy of the sexes by his persistent "feminolatry," the American Adam is no longer capable of keeping the American Eve "in her place." "The peculiar notions of personal independence indulged in by the women's rights' ladies in America," declared the Victorian writer James D. Burn in 1855, "have been the means of placing a great portion of the fabric of female society in a false position. Woman was evidently assigned to be the companion of man, and as he is stronger, both mentally and physically, it follows as a necessary consequence that he is a power above her. . . . The class of ladies I refer to take a different view of the matter; they are not content to hold the position Providence has placed them in as hand-maidens to the men, but they too must be rulers beyond the regions of the kitchen and nursery." Thanks to these "female notions of equality," he argued, the women of the United States regard domestic duties as demeaning, and so "it is a common thing for the man to do a considerable part of the slip-slop work. In the morning he lights the stove-fire, empties the slops, makes ready his own breakfast, and if his work lies at a distance he packs up his midday meal."

Complaints such as these recur with monotonous regularity in European descriptions of American society, especially during the nineteenth century. Many of Burn's objections were anticipated, for example, by Dickens' portrayal of the female inhabitants of the United States in *Martin Chuzzlewit*. From the formidable Mrs. Dawkins, "who held strong sentiments concerning the rights of women," to the philosophical Mrs. Brick and her friends, who take umbrage at a casual reference to their "family duties at home," virtually every woman Martin encounters in the New World regards domestic matters with undisguised contempt. As an American friend informs Martin after his faux pas in the Brick household, "domestic drudgery was far beneath the exalted range of these Philosophers, and . . . the chances were a hundred to one that not one of [them] could perform the easiest woman's work for herself, or make the simplest article of dress for any of her children." No wonder that America was so sparsely populated, concluded George Steevens over fifty years later. The "deliberate refusal of pampered women to assume the responsibilities of motherhood" could hardly fail to keep the birthrate down.

A still more common criticism of American women has to do not so much with their reluctance to play the traditional female role as with their readiness to assume the traditional male one. As we might expect, this proclivity is felt to be most threatening in the context of the sexual relationship itself. "Generally speaking," claimed Burn, "the male and female members of the human family are mutually drawn to each other; but as the greater attraction is vested in the female, the men . . . are constantly being drawn to their rocky charms by an irresistible force. This law of human magnetism seems in some measure to be reversed in America; the active power of attraction is changed, and instead of the lovely dears containing their vestal souls in patience, they frequently find themselves impelled to rush into the arms of their other halves." Indeed, ever since Captain John Smith was accosted by thirty naked Indian maidens crying "Love you not me? Love you not me?" the sexual aggressiveness of American women has been a byword in European literature. Here, for instance, is the hero of Kingsley Amis' *One Fat Englishman* on his first date with the wife of an American colleague: "She had seized his jacket and the shirt inside it and some of his arms inside that and held him in a surprisingly firm grip. 'Just relax honey. . . .' To his slight astonishment she was hauling, or levering, him to the ground, and he had just enough time to decide that he would prefer to be sitting down before he did so. American women seemed entirely without finesse. He preferred frank submission to frank pursuit. . . ." For once in his life Roger Micheldene has been treated as a sex object.

The other supposedly male prerogative that the American female has been accused of usurping is the exercise of moral authority in the home. In order to ensure that his children retained no trace of their European origins, Gorer argues, the immigrant father deliberately encouraged them to reject him. Since the mother retained her importance as the source of love, food, and succor, she "could not be rejected as the father had been, nor did public attitudes demand that she should be; and so the mother became the dominant parent in the American family, almost, as it were, by default." As a result, Gorer concluded, the American conscience "is predominantly feminine. Owing to the major role played by the mother in disciplining the child, in rewarding and punishing it, many more aspects of the mother than of the father become incorporated. Duty and Right Conduct become feminine figures." One could hardly wish for a better commentary on Ralph Touchett's relationship with his parents in Henry James' novel *The Portrait of a Lady* (1881): "His father, as he had often said to himself, was the more motherly; his mother, on the other hand, was paternal, and even, according to the slang of the day, gubernatorial." In parenthood as in courtship, the men and women of America appear to have switched roles.

A Nation of Amazons

Behind many of the passages I have just been quoting, one can detect the presence of a figure that has haunted the male imagination from the beginning of Western literature, the figure of the Amazon. And as a matter of fact, she appears very early in European accounts of the New World. While he was exploring Hispaniola, Columbus reported in his "Letter to Santangel," he was told that the island of Matinino (the modern Martinique) was inhabited entirely by a tribe of women who "engage in no feminine occupation, but use bows and arrows of cane, like those already mentioned," and who "arm and protect themselves with plates of copper, of which they have much." To a classically trained scholar like Peter Martyr, the parallel with the Greek island of Lesbos was inescapable. The men of the neighboring islands, he wrote in his amplification of Columbus' narrative, are permitted to visit Matinino once a year for breeding purposes "as in ancient history the Thracians crossed to the island of Lesbos inhabited by the Amazons."

Fortunately for him perhaps, Columbus never succeeded in landing on Matinino, though he did encounter female warriors elsewhere in the New World, on one occasion with fatal results: according to Peter Martyr, a woman armed with bow and arrows killed one member of the Admiral's crew and severely wounded another on the island of Santa Cruz. Nor was this an isolated incident if the travel literature of the sixteenth century is to be believed. In his *Four Voyages*, for example, Vespucci gave the following account of his landing in South America: "As soon as we landed [the natives] sent many of their women to talk with us. But even the women did not trust us sufficiently. While we were waiting for them to approach, we decided to send them one of our young men who was very strong and agile; and then, that the women might be the less fearful, the rest of us embarked in our small boats. The young man advanced and mingled among the women; they all stood around him, and touched and stroked him, wondering greatly at him. At this point a woman came down from the hill carrying a big club. When she reached the place where the young man was standing, she struck him such a heavy blow from behind that he immediately fell to the ground dead. The rest of the women at once seized him and dragged him by the feet up the mountain. . . . There the women, who had killed the youth before our eyes, were now cutting him in pieces, showing us the pieces, roasting them at a large fire which they had made, and eating them." After reading such episodes it is not hard to understand what prompted the English poet Edmund Spenser to describe the conquest of the New World as a battle between the sexes. "Joy to those warlike women," he declared in *The Faerie Queene*, "which so long":

> Can from all men so rich a kingdom hold.
> And shame on you, O men, which boast your strong
> And valiant hearts, in thoughts less hard and bold,
> Yet quail in conquest of that land of gold.

It may well be no accident that the hero of Kafka's *Amerika* thought the Statue of Liberty was holding not a torch but a sword!

Mr. America

As we have seen, the women of Matinino admitted men to their island only once a year. In the rest of the New World, however, the two sexes evidently lived together, and it must have occurred to many a sixteenth-century European to wonder how the American Amazons treated their own menfolk. Vespucci's account of domestic life on the other side of the Atlantic provided a rather alarming answer. "Their women," he wrote, "being very lustful, cause the private parts of their husbands to swell up to such a huge size that they appear deformed and disgusting; and this is accomplished by a certain device of theirs, the biting of certain poisonous animals. And in consequence of this many [of the men] lose their organs which break through lack of attention, and they remain eunuchs."

The victims of the castrating American female have thronged the pages of European descriptions of this country ever since. Whether they are metaphorical eunuchs like Mr. Joyboy in Waugh's *The Loved One* or virginal schoolboys like Alden Pyle in *The Quiet American*, the men of the New World have repeatedly been accused of sexual inadequacy by the men of the Old. According to several eighteenth-century commentators, for instance, the sparseness of America's population was directly attributable to the insensibility of its male inhabitants to "the charms of beauty and the power of love," as William Robertson maintained. "They are cold in love," declared Cornelius de Pauw, "and utterly indifferent toward women." "Men who have little more hair than eunuchs cannot abound in generating principles," explained the

Abbé Raynal. "The blood of these people is watery and cold. The males sometimes have milk in their breasts. Hence arises their tardy inclination to the [opposite] sex."

Twentieth-century commentators characteristically attribute the phenomenon to psychological rather than physiological factors, but they rarely seem to question the phenomenon itself. To take a comparatively recent example, Gorer is very concerned in *The American People* to account for "the deep ambivalence" which he believes "most American men feel toward women." The "relatively dominant position of the mother in the American family," he argues, has produced in her sons "a predominantly feminine conscience," and since every American man consequently "has a feminine component in his personality, there is always a deeply hidden doubt concerning his own masculinity." Nowhere, however, does Gorer attempt to demonstrate the existence of the syndrome he purports to be explaining. The "very strong ambivalence American men feel toward women" is simply taken for granted in his study.

The general impression that emerges from the foregoing passages has been summarized with admirable clarity by Müller-Freienfels. In America, he writes, "the difference between the sexes is not so great as it is— or used to be—with us. Women do not constitute a downtrodden caste; they are so dominant that some Europeans have spoken of gynocracy. Even the young girl behaves with an independence which is startling to the European, and seems to him 'unfeminine'; and conversely, he often detects feminine traits in the American man." It is not too difficult to guess what role the European may consequently be tempted to see himself playing in such a situation. Secure in his own sexual identity, he fondly believes that he can offer the frustrated American woman nothing less than a chance to rediscover her lost femininity.

The Subjugation of Columbia

Henry James' great novel *The Portrait of a Lady* reveals the tragic consequences that ensue when these myths are taken seriously. The "lady" of the title is Isabel Archer, a young American woman who has gone to Europe with her aunt Mrs. Touchett in order to broaden her experience. Once there she brings to bear on her new environment a point of view which she herself describes as "thoroughly American," so much so, indeed, that her Europeanized cousin Ralph Touchett amuses himself "with calling her 'Columbia' and accusing her of a patriotism so fervid that it scorched." Isabel, it seems clear from the outset, is intended as an epitome of the American woman.

Her national identity emerges particularly clearly in her refusal to conform to European notions of female subservience. "American girls

Americca by Etienne Delaune.

were used to a great deal of deference," Ralph recalls shortly after her arrival, and Isabel proves to be no exception. "Like the majority of American girls," James points out later, "Isabel had been encouraged to express herself; her remarks had been attended to; she had been expected to have emotions and opinions." So when her first European suitor, Lord Warburton, treats her as if she were the pretty little nincompoop he obviously expects her to be, she cannot resist laying a trap for him. First she asks him a series of deliberately artless questions, and then, when he has made the mistake of taking them at face value, she punctures his condescension by remarking: "It's a pity you can't see me in my warpaint and feathers, . . . if I had known how kind you are to the poor savages, I would have brought over my national costume." No Pocahontas she, as Lord Warburton is soon forced to admit. "I am very much afraid of it," he confesses in a subsequent conversation, "that mind of yours." To a European man who has been as completely taken in by the contemptuous version of the myth as Lord Warburton evidently has, an American woman of any real intelligence could hardly fail to seem rather intimidating.

It is her "mind," incidentally, which distinguishes Isabel Archer from her famous Jamesian predecessor, Daisy Miller. For although both women display an almost total disregard for the conventions governing "feminine" behavior in European society, only Isabel appears to have made a conscious choice to challenge the accepted norms. As she explains to Mrs. Touchett when the older woman has rebuked her for offering "to sit alone with the gentlemen at night," she would always prefer to know "the things one shouldn't do" in Europe. "So as to do them?" inquires her aunt. "So as to choose," replies Isabel. Unlike Daisy, therefore, she can flout convention without appearing to be merely gauche. If she breaks the rules, it is because she disapproves of them, not because she is unaware of their existence.

Yet despite her undoubted intelligence, there is one crucial respect in which Isabel is quite as innocent as the naive young girl whose social indiscretions created such a stir in the earlier story: she has not yet tasted the forbidden fruit. No one realizes this more clearly than Ralph. The ghost which haunts the Touchett household, he tells his cousin, cannot be seen "by a young, happy, innocent person like you." "I told you just now I was very fond of knowledge," she retorts. "Yes, of happy knowledge—of pleasant knowledge," he concedes. "But you haven't suffered, and you are not made to suffer." Isabel, James himself observes in the next chapter, "had a fixed determination to regard the world as a place of brightness, of free expansion, of irresistible action; she thought it would be detestable to be afraid or ashamed. She had an infinite hope that she should never do anything wrong. . . . she had seen very little of the evil of the world." In her imagination, at least, the American Eve is still living in the garden of Eden. In fact, of course, she has left it behind her on the other side of the Atlantic.

Perhaps the most striking expression of her innocence is the extraordinarily high value she places on her "personal independence," a phrase that accompanies her through the novel like a Wagnerian *leitmotiv*. Lacking as she does any sense of moral limitation, Isabel believes that her liberty is total. "The world lay all before her—she could do whatever she chose." Her American suitor Caspar Goodwood, who in accordance with James' view of his fellow countrymen is an energetic captain of industry, thus appeals to Isabel's most treasured conviction when he makes her what I have come to believe is the quintessential American offer, the offer of absolute freedom: "We can do absolutely as we please," he assures her. "To whom under the sun do we owe anything? What is it that holds us? ... Were we born to rot in misery— were we born to be afraid? I never knew *you* afraid! The world is all before us." But as the echo of the final lines of *Paradise Lost* reminds us, the world that lies before them is a fallen one. Whatever else it may be, Europe is no paradise.

On Isabel, however, it exerts a fatal attraction, and long before Goodwood delivers his last desperate appeal, she has fallen victim to the patronizing version of the myth in the person of Henry Osmond, the imperious representative of Europe. Strictly speaking, Osmond too is an American, but as all the other characters in the novel recognize he has lived abroad for so long that he has lost all traces of his original national identity. "He is an American," Ralph grudgingly admits to Lord Warburton, "but one forgets that, he is so little of one." Succumbing to the perennial temptation of the expatriate, Osmond has become more native than the natives. With his "immense esteem for tradition," his concern with keeping up appearances, and his passion for decorum, he is in danger of becoming a mere caricature of the cultivated European man of taste. "You say you don't know me," he tells Isabel at one point, "but when you do you will discover what a worship I have for propriety." "You are not conventional?" she inquires. "I like the way you utter that word!" he replies. "No, I am not conventional: I am convention itself." No wonder she regards him as the very incarnation of European culture. "She was to think of him," James informs us, "as he thought of himself—as the first gentleman in Europe. So it was that she had thought of him at first, and that indeed was the reason she had married him."

The reason he had married her was rather less high-minded: her fortune could support Osmond in the style to which he believed his good taste entitled him. But beneath his obvious financial interest in Isabel one can detect, I think, another motive at work. Goodwood had told her that "it is to make you independent that I want to marry you." Osmond seems to have precisely the opposite purpose in mind. For although there is nothing even remotely masculine about Isabel—James carefully diverts the Amazonian aspects of *femina Americana* onto her aggressive friend Henrietta Stackpole—Osmond clearly feels that there is something unbecoming about her intellectual independence. "Isabel has one great fault," he remarks after meeting her for the first time. "She has too many ideas." His self-appointed mission is to perform upon her the same mental operation that John Rolfe had aspired to perform upon Pocahontas, to transform her into a replica of his own mind, a mirror in which to admire his own rectitude, piety, and good taste:

> The real offense, as she ultimately perceived, was her having a mind of her own at all. Her mind was to be his—attached to his own like a small garden-plot to a deer-park. He would rake the soil gently and water the flowers; he would weed the beds and gather an occasional nosegay. It would be a pretty piece of property for a proprietor already far-reaching. He didn't wish her to be stupid. On the contrary, it was because she was clever that she had pleased him. But he expected her intelligence to operate altogether in his favour, and so far from desiring her mind to be a blank, he had flattered himself that it would be richly receptive. He had expected his wife to feel with him and for him, to enter into his opinions, his ambitions, his preferences.

In the firm belief that he is restoring her womanly identity to her, Osmond proposes to obliterate her national identity altogether. "To enter in these bonds is to be free," Donne had assured his "America" in the poem I quoted at the beginning of this chapter. To be the mistress of Europe, Isabel discovers on the contrary, is to enter into an ignominious form of cultural servitude, to become once again a mere colony.

By the time Isabel achieves this insight into her predicament, however, it is too late for her to change it. After rejecting all her other suitors in the name of freedom, she has voluntarily submitted herself to the most limiting and authoritarian male in the entire novel, and her puritanical sense of moral obligation forbids her to shirk the terrible consequences of her mistake. Henrietta may advise Goodwood with characteristic optimism, "Just you wait," but James has made it clear that there is nothing for him to wait for. The American Eve has lost her innocence, and there is no going back to Eden.

EPILOGUE

THROUGHOUT THE FOREGOING DISCUSSION I have attempted, not always successfully, to remain at a certain distance from the material I have been analyzing. This study would not be complete, however, if I did not confront a question which has arisen in one form or another whenever I have lectured on these issues, namely, where do I stand myself? The most accurate answer would probably be, somewhere in the middle of the Atlantic. For strictly speaking I am at the moment neither a European nor an American but a European in the process of becoming an American. As a result, preparing this book has been for me a kind of cultural rite of passage, an opportunity to reassess the extraordinary conglomeration of myths and prejudices which I brought with me to this country when I first arrived in 1963. Most if not all of them, I can now recognize, were at best grossly exaggerated. America is neither Utopia nor Whispering Glades; its characteristic values are neither an affront to human dignity nor an unqualified affirmation of human freedom; and its men are neither Caspar Goodwoods nor Alden Pyles, its women neither Lolitas nor Isabel Archers. The truth, as always, is infinitely more complex than the crude generalizations to which the human mind seems determined to reduce it.

Yet however inaccurate or oversimplified they may be, the images I have been describing cannot be dismissed as mere delusions. Justified or not, they are cultural facts. As I have tried to show, they have existed in the mind and literature of Europe ever since the age of the discoveries. To ignore them, therefore, is not only to run the risk of misinterpreting the policies which they have shaped; it is to acquiesce in what I argued in Chapter Three is the greatest delusion of all: the delusion that people understand each other perfectly.

READER'S GUIDE

A list of all the books that have been written about America by European authors would fill this entire volume. In the interest of brevity I have therefore confined myself to works that I found particularly useful in preparing the foregoing study. Many of them contain exhaustive bibliographies on virtually every aspect of the Old World's relationship with the New.

Primary Sources

Anthologies

Axtell, James, William J. Baker, and Orm Överland. *America Perceived*. West Haven, Conn.: Pendulum Press, 1974.

A four-volume series designed as a companion to The American People series. Each volume is devoted to a single century, beginning with the seventeenth, and the materials are grouped under such headings as "The Native Americans," "City Life," "A Nation of Immigrants," and "America Abroad."

Commager, Henry Steele. *America in Perspective*. New York: Random House, 1947.

A skillfully assembled collection of materials illustrating how the United States has been perceived by a wide variety of foreign commentators ranging from Michel-Guillaume de Crèvecoeur in the eighteenth century to Denis Brogan in the twentieth. Among the works I have cited from this anthology are: Matthew Arnold's *Civilization in the United States*, James Hannay's *From Dublin to Chicago*, Paul Bourget's *Outre-Mer, Impressions of America*, James D. Burn's *Three Years Among the Working Classes in the United States*, William Cobbett's *A Year's Residence in America*, Francis Lieber's *Letters to a Gentleman in Germany*, Salvador de Madariaga's *Americans Are Boys*, Richard Müller-Freienfels' *The Mysteries of the Soul*, Raoul de Roussy de Sales' *Love in America*, Philip Schaff's *A Sketch of the Political, Social, and Religious Character of the United States*, and George W. Steevens' *The Land of the Dollar*.

———— and Elmo Giordanetti. *Was America a Mistake?* Columbia, South Carolina: University of South Carolina Press, 1967.

An invaluable guide to the dispute analyzed by Gerbi (see listing under "Secondary Studies"), this book contains extracts from the writings of most of the major contributors to the eighteenth-century debate on the physical, moral, and cultural status of America. The four introductory chapters define the central issues with admirable clarity. Among works cited from this anthology are: George Louis Leclerc, Comte de Buffon's *Natural History*, the Abbé Corneille de Pauw's *Philosophical Investigations of the Americans*, and Dr. William Robertson's *History of America*.

Wright, Louis B. *The Elizabethans' America*. Cambridge, Mass.: Harvard University Press, 1965.

Collected and introduced by the distinguished historian of Renaissance culture, this anthology of letters, essays, tracts, and poems offers a broad spectrum of Elizabethan opinions about the New World.

Fictional Treatments

Amis, Kingsley. *One Fat Englishman*. New York: Harcourt Brace, 1963.

Based at least in part on the author's experiences at Princeton University, this novel appears at first to be an ill-tempered attack on American life and manners. The real object of Amis' satire, however, is the novel's anti-American protagonist, Roger Micheldene.

Dickens, Charles. *Martin Chuzzlewit*. London: Chapman and Hall, 1844.

The American chapters in Dickens' great study of human egotism and hypocrisy are closely related to his earlier account of this country in his *American Notes*. After attempting to make a new life for himself in the American "Eden," Martin returns to England a changed man.

Greene, Graham. *The Quiet American*. London: Heinemann, 1955.

Inspired by Greene's encounter with an American attached to an economic aid mission in Vietnam in the early 1950s, this novel has frequently been misinterpreted as a prophetic denunciation of American foreign policy. Its true subject, I have argued, is the threat which the innocent pose to a fallen world.

James, Henry. *The Portrait of a Lady*. London: Macmillan, 1881.

By the time James wrote this novel he had lived in England for five years. With his sensibility delicately poised between the cultures of the Old World and the New, he created in Isabel Archer a poignant portrait of American independence slowly yielding to European domination.

Kafka, Franz. *Amerika*. Translated by Willa and Edwin Muir. London: George Routledge, 1938.

Originally published in German in 1927, Kafka's nightmarish account of Karl Rossman's adventures in New York and the surrounding countryside offers a penetrating insight into the nature of the immigrant experience.

More, Sir Thomas. *Utopia*. Translated by H.V.S. Ogden. New York: Appleton-Century-Crofts, 1949.

Written in 1515 and 1516, More's famous account of an ideal state was first translated from Latin into English by Ralph Robinson in 1551. It offers a unique insight into the way in which the discovery of America affected the imagination of sixteenth-century Europe.

Nabokov, Vladimir. *Lolita*. Paris: Olympia Press, 1955.

Humbert Humbert's notorious account of his affair with a young American "nymphet" is, among other things, a brilliant critique of the literary and psychological assumptions his creator attributes to the American reading public.

Waugh, Evelyn. *The Loved One*. Boston: Little, Brown, 1948.

The grotesque story of a young English poet's encounter with Los Angeles and its "great necropolis," Whispering Glades, the fictional equivalent of Forest Lawn.

Nonfictional Treatments

Beauvoir, Simone de. *America Day by Day*. Translated by Patrick Dudley. London: G. Duckworth, 1952.

Originally published in French in 1948, de Beauvoir's journal provides a graphic record of the impression this country made upon her when she visited it for the first time.

Bradford, Governor William. *Of Plymouth Plantation*. Edited with an introduction by William T. Davis. New York: Barnes and Noble, 1946.

The classic description of the Pilgrims' experiences in New England from 1620 to 1646 by the colony's second governor.

Brogan, Denis W. *The American Character*. New York: Knopf, 1944. Excerpts reprinted in Commager. *America in Perspective*.

A sympathetic and informed account of American character and institutions by a British professor of political science who served as head of the American division of the BBC during World War II.

Bruckberger, R.L. *Image of America*. Translated by C.G. Paulding and Virgilia Peterson. New York: Viking Press, 1959.

The major thesis of this provocative tract by the French Dominican priest, artist, theologian, and man of letters is that America will prove to be the salvation of Europe.

Columbus, Christopher. "The Letter to Santangel." Translated by Cecil Jane. *The Journal of Christopher Columbus*. London: Blond, 1968.

Columbus' first-hand account of his first voyage to the New World. Translated into Latin and Italian, it achieved wide circulation in Europe during the first half of the sixteenth century.

Cooper, Susan. *Behind the Golden Curtain*. New York: Scribners, 1965.

A lively and provocative inquiry into American life and manners which argues that the United States is gradually being isolated from the rest of the world by its own economic and cultural self-sufficiency.

Crèvecoeur, Michel-Guillaume de. *Letters from an American Farmer*. Edited by Ernest Rhys. New York: Dutton, 1912.

One of the most famous and perceptive accounts of the American character ever to be written by a European. Originally published in 1782, it has frequently been reprinted and anthologized.

Dickens, Charles. *American Notes*. Edited with an introduction by G.K. Chesterton. New York: Dutton, 1970.

Written shortly after his first visit to America in 1842, this rambling account of Dickens' impressions is a fascinating commentary not only on nineteenth-century America but also on the novel that Dickens published two years later, *Martin Chuzzlewit*.

Gorer, Geoffrey. *The American People*. Revised edition. New York: Norton, 1964.

A stimulating and often infuriating study of American national character which attempts to demonstrate that the key to understanding the people of the United States is "the individual rejection of the European father as a model and a moral authority, which every second-generation American had to perform."

Hakluyt, Richard. *A Discourse of Western Planting*. Edited by Charles Deane. Cambridge, Mass.: John Wilson and Son, 1877.

A passionate plea for the colonization of North America, written by the principal Elizabethan advocate of the exploration and settlement of the New World.

————. *The Principal Navigations, Voyages, Traffics, and Discoveries of the English Nation*. Edited with an introduction by John Masefield. New York: Dutton, 1910.

The greatest single collection ever made of Elizabethan travel literature. Hakluyt's work contains virtually all the major English accounts of the New World written before the publication of the revised edition of his anthology in 1598, including George Best's account of Sir Martin Frobisher's voyages and Philip Amadas and Arthur Barlow's letter to Sir Walter Raleigh.

James, Henry. *The American Scene*. Edited with an introduction by Leon Edel. Bloomington: Indiana University Press, 1968.

Written soon after James returned to the United States from a self-imposed European exile of almost a quarter of a century, this panoramic series of reflective sketches of the American landscape offers a unique and sometimes deeply moving analysis of a painful homecoming.

Martyr, Peter. *The New World*. Translated by Francis A. MacNutt. New York: Burt Franklin, 1970.

Divided into eight "decades," this work is one of the earliest and most influential histories of the Spanish exploration of the New World. The first decade, describing Columbus' exploits in Hispaniola, was published in 1511. Richard Eden issued the first English translation in 1555.

Montaigne, Michel Eyquem de. "On Cannibals." Translated by William Hazlitt. New York: Worthington, 1888.

Perhaps the most enlightened European response to the New World to be written in the sixteenth century, this essay influenced many subsequent Renaissance writers including Shakespeare.

———. "On Coaches." Translated by William Hazlitt (same edition as above).

This essay was well known to John Dryden, who incorporated several of its themes into his seventeenth-century drama set in the New World, *The Indian Emperor*.

Revel, Jean-François. *Without Marx or Jesus*. Translated by J.F. Bernard. New York: Doubleday, 1970.

Subtitled "The New American Revolution Has Begun," this analysis of American dissent reveals that for many European thinkers the New World is still the standard by which the Old should judge itself.

Santayana, George. *Character and Opinion in the United States*. New York: Norton, 1967.

This thoughtful collection of essays on the theme of American idealism was originally published in 1920 after Santayana had returned to Europe from Harvard University, where he taught philosophy for thirteen years.

Smith, Captain John. *The General History of Virginia*. Selections edited by John Lankford in *Captain John Smith's America*. New York: Harper and Row, 1967.

Described by his twentieth-century editor as "one of the first Englishmen to see America as more than a get-rich-quick scheme," John Smith provided his Renaissance contemporaries with a vivid and detailed account of life in the first English colony to be established in the New World.

Tocqueville, Alexis de. *Democracy in America*. Edited by J.P. Mayer and Max Lerner. New York: Harper and Row, 1966.

A classic study of the American social and political system in which the great French thinker examined the workings of the democratic principle in virtually every aspect of the life of this country.

Trollope, Frances. *Domestic Manners of the Americans*. Edited with an introduction by Donald Smalley. New York: Vintage, 1960.

Published ten years before Dickens' *American Notes*, this fascinating picture of mid-nineteenth-century America by the mother of the novelist Anthony Trollope was very popular in England but was universally execrated in the United States. Smalley's excellent introduction provides a useful historical background.

Vespucci, Amerigo. *The New World*. Translated by George T. Northrup. Princeton: Princeton University Press, 1916.

Originally published in Latin in 1503 this influential work was translated into English, Italian, German, Dutch, and Portuguese during the next twelve years. It portrays the New World in a considerably less attractive light than Columbus' "Letter to Santangel."

―――. *The Four Voyages* (same edition as above).

Sometimes referred to as "the Soderini letter," Vespucci's longer and more detailed account of his discoveries was first published in Italian in 1505 and subsequently translated into German. It provided Sir Thomas More with the fictional framework for his *Utopia* as well as many of the individual details.

Visual Treatments

Honour, Hugh. *The European Vision of America*. Kent, Ohio: Kent State University Press, 1976.

The illustrated catalogue of the brilliant exhibition at the National Gallery of Art in Washington, D.C. Organized by the Cleveland Museum of Art in collaboration with the National Gallery of Art and the Réunion des Musées Nationaux, Paris, it offers a comprehensive survey of European portrayals of the New World from the fifteenth century to the twentieth. Hugh Honour is the exhibition's guest curator.

―――. *The New Golden Land: European Images of America from the Discoveries to the Present Time*. New York: Pantheon Books, 1976.

A most readable account of the way in which America has been represented and misrepresented in both the art and literature of Europe from the time of its discovery onwards. Richly illustrated and amply documented, this is perhaps the finest single work on the subject yet to appear in print.

Lehner, Ernst and Johanna. *How They Saw the New World*. New York: Tudor, 1966.

A collection of Renaissance woodcuts, paintings, and maps of the New World, its flora and fauna, its inhabitants, and its discoverers.

Lorant, Stefan. *The New World: The First Pictures of America*. New York: Duell Sloan and Pearce, 1946.

An annotated edition of John White's watercolors, made in Virginia in 1585, and of Théodor de Bry's engravings (made after White's watercolors) as well as the paintings of Jacques le Moyne de Morgues, who came to Florida with the Huguenots in 1564. Lorant also prints some contemporary accounts of the New World, including Thomas Hariot's "Brief and True Report" (1588) and Ralph Lane's report to Sir Walter Raleigh on conditions in Virginia.

Secondary Studies

Berger, Max. *The British Traveller in America, 1836-1860*. New York: P.S. King and Staples, 1943.

A comprehensive summary of the impressions which British travelers of the mid-nineteenth century formed of the United States. See the companion studies by Jane Mesick and Richard L. Rapson below.

Elliott, J.H. *The Old World and the New: 1492-1650*. Cambridge: Cambridge University Press, 1970.

A brilliant and concise analysis of the cultural, economic, and political relationships between America and Europe in the Renaissance by one of England's leading historians.

Gerbi, Antonello. *The Dispute of the New World*. Translated by Jeremy Moyle. Pittsburgh: University of Pittsburgh Press, 1973.

A monumental study of the great debate which took place in Europe during the eighteenth and nineteenth centuries on the physical, moral, and cultural status of the New World.

Jones, Howard Mumford. *O Strange New World*. New York: Viking, 1965.

Currently available in a paperback edition, this prize-winning treatment of the formative years of American culture offers an authoritative review of the relationship between the Old World and the New up to the middle of the nineteenth century.

Mesick, Jane. *The English Traveler in America, 1785-1835.* New York: Columbia University Press, 1922.

The first in a series of three works concerned with the reactions of British travelers to the American scene. The subsequent studies by Max Berger and Richard L. Rapson continue the investigation as far as the mid-twentieth century.

Rapson, Richard L. *Britons View America.* Seattle: University of Washington Press, 1971.

The third in a series of studies initiated by Jane Mesick. Rapson's volume covers the years 1860 to 1935 and treats such topics as the American character, women, children and parents, religion, and education.

Rowse, A.L. *The Elizabethans and America.* London: Macmillan, 1959.

Originally delivered as the Trevelyan Lectures in Cambridge, this lively account of the British encounter with the New World in the sixteenth and early seventeenth centuries concludes with a concise survey of the way in which America was portrayed in Elizabethan literature.

Other Works Cited

Antin, Mary. *The Promised Land.* Boston: Houghton Mifflin Co., 1912.

Bacon, Sir Francis. *The New Atlantis,* "Of Plantations," "Of Goodness and Goodness of Nature." Cited from Sidney Warhaft. *Francis Bacon: A Selection of His Works.* Toronto: Macmillan, 1965.

Best, George. *A True Discourse of the Late Voyages of Discovery.* Cited from J. William Hebel, Hoyt H. Hudson et al. *Prose of the English Renaissance.* New York: Appleton-Century-Crofts, 1952.

Bingham, Richard. "If Honor and Reward." Quoted in Louis B. Wright. *The Elizabethans' America* (listed under "Anthologies").

Chapman, George. *Eastward Ho.* Quoted in A.L. Rowse. *The Elizabethans and America* (listed under "Secondary Studies").

――――. *De Guiana Carmen Epicum.* Quoted in Robert R. Cawley. *The Voyagers and Elizabethan Drama.* Boston: Heath, 1938.

Dante Alighieri. *The Divine Comedy.* Translated by Laurence Binyon. *The Portable Dante.* New York: Viking, 1947.

Donne, John. "Love's Progress," "To His Mistress Going to Bed," "The Sun Rising." From *John Donne: The Elegies and The Songs and Sonnets.* Edited by Helen Gardner. Oxford: Clarendon Press, 1965.

――――. "A Sermon Preached to the Honorable Company of the Virginian Plantation." From *The Sermons of John Donne.* Volume IV. Edited by George R. Potter and Evelyn M. Simpson. Berkeley: University of California Press, 1959.

Drayton, Michael. "To the Virginian Voyage." Quoted in Louis B. Wright. *The Elizabethans' America* (listed under "Anthologies").

Fletcher, Francis. *The World Encompassed.* March of America Facsimile Series. Number 11. Ann Arbor: University of Michigan Microfilms, 1966.

Grenville, Sir Richard, Sr. "In Praise of Sea-faring Men." Quoted in Samuel E. Morison. *The European Discovery of America.* Oxford: Clarendon Press, 1971.

Hawthorne, Nathaniel. *The Marble Faun.* Edited by Murray Krieger. New York: New American Library, 1961.

Keats, John. "Lines to Fanny." Cited from H. Buxton Forman. *The Poetical Works of John Keats.* London: Oxford University Press, 1908.

Machiavelli, Niccolò. *The Discourses*. Translated by Max Lerner. New York: Random House, 1950.

———. *The Prince*. Translated by T.G. Bergin. New York: Appleton-Century-Crofts, 1947.

McCarthy, Mary. *The Stones of Florence*. New York: Harcourt Brace, 1959.

O'Gorman, Edmundo. *The Invention of America*. Bloomington: Indiana University Press, 1961.

Ovid. *Metamorphoses*. Translated with an introduction by Mary M. Innes. London: Penguin, 1955.

Petrarch, Francis. *The Canzoniere*. Translated by Anna Maria Armi. *Petrarch: Sonnets and Songs*. New York: Grosset and Dunlap, 1968.

Rastell, John. *The Interlude of the Four Elements*. From *A Select Collection of Old English Plays*. Edited by W. Carew Hazlitt. London: Reeves and Turner, 1874.

Rolfe, John. "Letter to Sir Thomas Dale." Quoted in Louis B. Wright. *The Elizabethans' America* (listed under "Anthologies").

Shakespeare, William. *Twelfth Night, Hamlet, The Tempest*. *William Shakespeare: The Complete Works*. Edited by Peter Alexander. London: Collins, 1951.

Shaw, George Bernard. *Back to Methuselah*. Cited from Penguin Edition. Harmondsworth, Middlesex: Penguin, 1954.

Shelley, Percy. *The Revolt of Islam*. Cited from Thomas Hutchinson. *The Complete Poetical Works of Percy Bysshe Shelley*. London: Oxford University Press, 1917.

Spenser, Edmund. *The Faerie Queene*. Edited by J.C. Smith and E. de Selincourt. *The Poetical Works of Edmund Spenser*. London: Oxford University Press, 1912.

Tasso, Torquato. *Jerusalem Delivered*. Translated by Edward Fairfax. New York: Capricorn, 1963.

Waldseemüller, Martin. *Introduction to Cosmography*. Translated by Joseph Fischer and Franz von Weiser. March of America Facsimile Series. Number 2. Ann Arbor: University of Michigan Microfilms, 1966.

West, Nathanael. *The Day of the Locust*. Edited by Richard B. Gehman. New York: Bantam, 1975.

INDEX

Adam and Eve, metaphor of, 12
  and denial of mortality, 40
  and geography, 64
  immigrant relives innocence of, 76,
    77
  natives compared to, 3, 4, 86
  and New World as wilderness, 27
  and sexual behavior, 40, 113, 120,
    121
Amadas, Philip, 24, 88
Amazons, 115–16, 121
America at Home (Low), 105
America Day by Day (Beauvoir), 17,
  70, 72
America in Perspective (Commager),
  47
American Notes (Dickens)
  on America as wilderness, 26–27
  on anti-authoritarianism, 68
  on settlers, 92, 95–96
  on unreality, 34–35
American People, The (Gorer)
  on anti-authoritarianism, 67
  on assimilation, 14–15
  on attitudes toward death, 41
  on men's attitudes toward women,
    117
American Scene, The (James)
  excess reflected in hotel, 72
  impermanence of buildings, 33–34
  openness of architecture, 53
  relation of sexes, 112
American Spectator, The
  (Mandrillon), 61
American Way of Death, The
  (Mitford), 37
Amerika (Kafka), 79–83
Amis, Kingsley
  on architectural openness, 46
  on excess, 71
  on spontaneity, 49
  on women, 114
Anti-authoritarianism, 66–70
Antin, Mary, 76
Architecture
  excess in, 71
  impermanence in, 32–35
  openness in, 43–47, 53–54, 61

Arizona, 14
Arnold, Matthew, 31, 111
Aspern Papers, The (James), 54
Authenticity, 32

Back to Methuselah (Shaw), 79
Bacon, Sir Francis
  on natives, 85
  New Atlantis compared to More's
    Utopia, 11, 12
  on settlers, 95
  and U.S. as "citizen of the world",
    15
Baffin Island, gold rush, 23
Barlow, Captain Arthur, 24, 88
Beauvoir, Simone de
  on America as hope, 17
  on dynamism, 70, 72
  on openness, 47
Best, George, 63
Bingham, Captain, 91–92
Blake, William, 26
Boston, Massachusetts, 34–35
Bourget, Paul, 14, 71
Bradford, William, 18
Brod, Max, 81
Brooks, Van Wyck, 111
Bruckberger, R. L., 17, 65, 75–76
Buchan, John, 47
Buffon, Comte de, 24–25, 26
Burke, Edmund, 68–69
Burn, James D., 113, 114

California, 14, 88
  Hollywood, 31, 37, 38
  Los Angeles, 35, 38
Candor, reverence for, 47–49
  feigned, 56
  in marriage, 52–53
Cannibalism, 89, 116
Canzoniere (Petrarch), 106
Catholic Church, 77, 91
Chapman, George, 18–19, 107
*Character and Opinion in the United
  States* (Santayana), 15, 51
Chastellux, Marquis de, 25
Child-rearing, 67, 68, 117
Civilization in the United States

ABOUT THE AUTHOR

Until 1963, J. Martin Evans was himself looking at America through a European's eyes. A native of Cardiff, Professor Evans spent his early years in South Wales. He was drafted into the Royal Air Force at the age of eighteen and spent the next two years learning Russian at the Joint Services Language School in Cambridge University. After completing his military service Evans was admitted to Jesus College, Oxford, gaining his AB in English literature in 1958. Evans completed his doctoral dissertation on Milton's *Paradise Lost* in 1963, receiving his PhD from Oxford's Merton College. In the same year he and his Swiss wife Mariella immigrated to the United States, where Evans had accepted an appointment as assistant professor in the English Department at Stanford. He was made an associate professor in 1968 and a full professor in 1975.

A noted Milton scholar, Professor Evans has authored several books, among them *Paradise Lost and the Genesis Tradition.* He is currently in England doing research at Oxford on another book under a fellowship from the National Endowment for the Humanities. A passionate Italophile, Professor Evans will soon begin his third tour of duty at the Stanford Overseas Campus in Florence. He has also taught at the Stanford Overseas Campus in Britain.